DISCOVER
TORCH
ENAMELING

GET STARTED WITH
25 SURE-FIRE
PROJECTS

Kalmbach Books
21027 Crossroads Circle
Waukesha, Wisconsin 53186
www.JewelryAndBeadingStore.com

Numbered step-by-step photos by the author. Author photo, p. 111, by Susan Scherrman. All other photography © 2016 Kalmbach Books except where otherwise noted.

The jewelry designs in *Discover Torch Enameling* are the copyrighted property of the author, and they may not be taught or sold without permission. Please use them for your education and personal enjoyment only.

Please follow appropriate health and safety measures when working with materials and equipment. Some general guidelines are presented in this book, but always read and follow manufacturers' instructions.

Every effort has been made to ensure the accuracy of the information presented; however, the publisher is not responsible for any injuries, losses, or other damages that may result from the use of the information in this book.

Published in 2016
20 19 18 17 16   1 2 3 4 5

Manufactured in China

ISBN: 978-1-62700-324-7
EISBN: 978-1-62700-325-4

Editor: Erica Swanson
Book Design: Lisa Bergman
Photographer: William Zuback

Library of Congress Control Number: 2016931487

DISCOVER TORCH ENAMELING

GET STARTED WITH 25 SURE-FIRE PROJECTS

STEVEN JAMES

KB
KALMBACH BOOKS

WAUKESHA, WI

CONTENTS

CHAPTER 1: BEYOND THE BASICS

CHAPTER 2: FANTASTIC FINISHES

CHAPTER 3: WORKING WITH WIRE

CHAPTER 4: MANIPULATING METAL

CHAPTER 5: CREATING CONNECTIONS

PLAY!

It's my favorite action verb, hands down. It's also how I've always approached arts and crafts. I am grateful to have grown up with parents and teachers who encouraged me to have fun and play. Well, most of the time. They must have already known what I eventually figured out. Play is about more than just fun. It's also about discovery, of yourself and the world around you. Sadly, for adults, play doesn't always make the schedule in our "work, work, work" culture. We rarely allow ourselves enough opportunities to have fun. So please think of this book as your invitation.

I encourage you to discover all torch enameling can offer you as a designer. The combination of color, shapes, and textures will yield amazing and unlimited results. Play with these projects and make them your own. Pick colors that speak to you, choose shapes that reflect your personality—combine project techniques to produce something never before seen. Go on—play!

Yes, there are a few rules. We are, after all, playing with fire, and we all know how the old saying goes. So follow the techniques and take precautions to play safely. But then "go wild."

If you get stuck, don't worry. That's part of the fun. Take a break or try a new approach. If you get REALLY stuck, just raise your hand. My day job is teaching children, so I've heard it all. Seriously, email me with any questions. I'm happy to help.

Finally, please keep in touch. Visit my website, macaroniandglitter.com. I absolutely love seeing what my students make, so be sure to send me photos of your amazing creations. My Instagram and Pinterest pages aren't going to fill themselves.

ARE YOU READY? IT'S PLAYTIME!

— Steven

BASICS

Tools and Materials

As much as I like to stress the importance of tapping into your imagination and letting your mind get into play mode, the truth is, this is only half of the torch-enameling equation. None of the fabulous projects you create would be possible without the right tools and materials. Tools help you make the magic happen.

In this section, I've listed what I consider to be a comprehensive set of tools for the beginning torch-enamel artist. For each of the projects in this book, you'll use a different combination of these tools. In some cases, you might need a specialized tool—which I will briefly introduce here, and discuss in more detail in the project description. As an instructor, I always encourage students to find affordable solutions for tools. Here are a few things I've learned in my torch enameling to help keep costs down.

Go with what you know. There are many established brands in the crafting industry and they are typically successful for a reason. Be open to trying new products and tools, but use the Internet and your crafting community to get recommendations. Make sure products are legit before you blow your budget on them.

Don't skimp on flame. As much as I like to save money when I can, I never cut costs with torches—and always buy the best one I can afford. The same goes for fuel. Why spend a lot of money on a torch, only to fill it with low-quality butane?

Avoid impulse shopping. As you begin to master different torch-enameling techniques, you'll likely find yourself geeking out on new tools you discover. I know I do. As tempting as some of the new-fangled tools might be, try to avoid spending loads of money on a tool you might only use once or twice. If you need a specific tool for something, consider a low-cost alternative.

Sharing is caring. Another way to keep costs down is by sharing tools and materials. If you have an enameling buddy or a circle of creative friends, consider building a collective toolbox for the materials you begin to acquire.

Get to know your tools and materials. Once you have a few projects under your belt, you'll begin to make connections between different tools and figure out how to take certain techniques even further by using these tools in new ways. This book is only the beginning!

KILN BRICK

The kiln brick is an essential element in the enameling process. It is your torch-enameling stage. Not only does it support the trivet, but the residual heat coming off of the brick can expedite the firing process. Kiln bricks are widely available at ceramic studios, but you can also order them online. Kiln bricks are extremely fragile and small pieces of the bricks can find their way into your enamel, so be sure to separate your firing station from your design area **[1]**.

TRIVET

The stainless-steel trivet is a required tool for enameling. It holds your copper in place while you fire it. Most of the projects in this book require a three-point star trivet sized at either 2-in. or 1½-in. You can find trivets in a variety of sizes, but bigger is not necessarily better, especially when working with smaller pieces of copper. As you begin to enamel, you'll notice the trivet will collect small amounts of fused glass—perhaps from spills or the urge to sift enamel onto the copper while it is on the trivet. You can remove fused glass with a quick squeeze of your bentnose pliers (wear safety glasses!) or file away enamel from the edges with an inexpensive diamond file **[2]**.

TORCH

There are two ways to fire enamel: in a kiln or with a torch. All of the projects in this book use a Max Flame torch, along with extremely refined, food-grade butane gas. A clean and pure butane gas helps keep your torch working correctly, so don't hesitate to spend a little more on the gas. In my classes, I've also encouraged students to work with larger torches such as the MAP-Pro BernzOmatic Hand Torch. A larger torch allows you to create bigger projects with larger copper pieces **[3]**.

When it comes to torch preference, it's all about your comfort level. If you've never worked with torches before, you might opt for a smaller handheld torch. With these, you can channel your inner Martha Stewart and get used to working with it by making crème brulee (I've got a killer recipe if you're interested!). Regardless of the torch you use, keep in mind the flame temperature needs to reach at least 1400 degrees Fahrenheit (760 degrees Celsius) to fuse the enamel to the copper. The torch will also be on for extended periods of time, so avoid buying a torch that could breakdown after very little use. Small, plastic economy-priced torches will not likely do the job.

COPPER BLANKS AND WIRE

Copper is my go-to metal for torch enameling. You can easily purchase copper blanks everywhere and I often use copper tubing and wire from the hardware store. I find that 18–22-gauge copper blanks are best, while I use 18–26 gauge copper wire. And it's no secret copper pennies minted before 1982 can also be used as a copper source, as they are pure copper **[4]**.

MAGAZINE SHEETS

The glossy sheets from your favorite magazine offer the perfect work surface for the sifting process. You can sift over a small piece of paper and then fold and return the extra enamel back to the bottle or the sifting cup. Do not be tempted to reuse sheets, unless you're working with the same color on multiple pieces. Enamels can mix easily and alter your finished design. When I work with multiple pieces in the same color, I will apply one color of enamel to all of the pieces at once. If by chance you do have a spill and contaminate colors, don't throw them away. Just use wthem as counterenamel for future projects **[5]**.

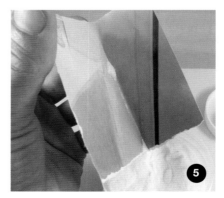

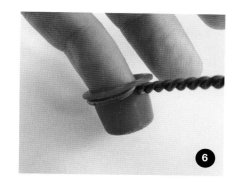

SIFTER

A sifter evenly distributes the enamel onto the surface of your metal. Much like trivets, sifters come in a variety of sizes, with different mesh screen sizes at the bottom of the cup. All of the projects in this book use 80-mesh enamel, which is a common measurement of ground enamels. I also prefer to use the smallest sifting cup possible—in this case, the 1/2-in. diameter sifter. As you are working with smaller projects, a smaller sifter is easier to control during the application process. To clean the sifter between applications, I use a large-head paintbrush or my pinky finger (I use a water bowl to rinse my finger after.) **[6]**.

SMALL PLASTIC BOTTLE OR "STILT"

Students often struggle moving the copper blank from the sifting sheet to the trivet. A small plastic bottle can serve as a stilt to allow you to use your fingers and grab the metal from the sides. Simply rest the blank on top of the lid, with a small edge protruding off of the side. This is a great tip for small pieces of copper or pieces of copper without holes! If you're worried about transferring the copper piece from the sifting sheet with fine-point tweezers, I encourage a few practice sessions with bare copper first.

DUST MASK

In classes, my students use a heavy-duty NIOSH-N95 dust mask. The dust mask is absolutely crucial to use when sifting your enamels. I don't find it necessary to wear a mask when firing a standard project, but there is no harm in keeping it on. The exception to this rule is when you are working with the in-flame projects,

immersing the metal into the enamel or sifting on to the metal during the firing process. In the book, you'll discover specific in-flame projects (the process in which you are immersing metal into the copper and placing it within the flame), requiring you to wear masks during the firing stage **[7]**.

SAFETY GLASSES

In addition to wearing a dust mask, you should also wear safety glasses—only when firing projects. When you fire in a cold room or if the glass becomes unstable as it cools down, there is always a risk of glass popping off of the metal. This is why wearing safety glasses is so important whenever you fire. If you are serious about torch enameling, a pair of Aura lens glasses is a great investment. They provide excellent protection from ultraviolet light, infrared light, and sodium flare **[8]**.

TITANIUM PICK

I use these tools when I work with tubes or metal pieces that don't fit on a traditional trivet. Don't be alarmed when small pieces of glass adhere to the pick. It is easy to remove the glass with a gentle squeeze from a pair of bentnose pliers. I often purchase my picks in sets, so I don't repeatedly use the same pick over and over again. A more basic use of the pick is as an aid for cleaning out a clogged hole in your metal. Specific projects in the book require you to use a titanium pick, but you can also use this tool with soldering projects as well, to move around soldered pieces before they set **[9]**.

BENTNOSE PLIERS

If you've taken a class from me, you know this is one of my favorite tools. My personal bentnose pliers are pretty beat up, as I use them exclusively for the enameling technique. I often use economy-priced pliers to pick up and move the trivets, as well as to remove the project from the trivet **[10]**.

TWEEZERS

I use two types of tweezers when I enamel. The smaller, fine-point tweezers are perfect for picking up projects off of the sifting surface and placing them on the trivet. (By the way, it is much easier to find the hole in the metal if you always position it at the 12 o'clock position.) I use heat-resistant, fiber-handled, cross-locking tweezers to hold metal for projects using the in-flame enameling technique. You'll find specific projects need one or the other, but it is a good idea to have both of these tools on hand. Neither type of tweezers has a good enough grip to securely hold and move the firing trivet, so resist the urge to use tweezers to do so.

PENNY BRITE (CITRIC ACID)

Removing firescale from copper can be done in several ways. Back in the day, I used Sparex No. 2, a pickling solution used in enameling and traditional metalsmithing. Once I discovered Penny Brite, a citric acid-based product, I set Sparex No. 2 aside. I appreciate Penny Brite as a natural, bio-degradable solution for removing firescale. When you add in a little elbow grease and an old toothbrush, you can work with gloved hands to clean your copper. In fact, you can clean the copper quite easily. I've also made my own Penny Brite (citric acid) "pickle" which doesn't need to be heated. It is a generous dollop of Penny Brite mixed with one cup of water. I often leave pieces in need of cleaning in the pickle bath while I work and let it work its magic! Always rinse your metal before you sift the enamel and check the punched holes to make sure you've removed all Penny Brite remnants **[11]**.

SCALEX

Some of the projects require you to work with exposed metal surfaces on projects that are partially enameled—such as the soldering projects. Scalex or ball-clay prevents firescale from forming on the surface of copper. It is a slurry-like ball clay and is paintable, so you can add it to specific sections of your copper. It is best to allow the Scalex to air dry to avoid cracking before you fire the project **[12]**.

KLYR-FIRE

Klyr-Fire is an organic adhesive that some people call a "holding agent," and in fact, is exactly what it does. It holds sifted enamel in place during the firing process. Some people use this adhesive with every project, but I tend to only use it for curved or dimensional work.

PAINTBRUSHES

It is helpful to have a couple of brushes for specific jobs. Paintbrushes with differently-sized bristle heads are important to use when applying enamel paint, Klyr-Fire, or Scalex. You might consider one brush exclusively used for Klyr-Fire and one brush exclusively used for Scalex. You'll also need smaller paintbrushes for finer details when using enameling paints (remember to always clean the brushes after use). I also use dry brushes with larger heads to clean out sifters between colors. These large-head brushes are only used to clean out sifters and not used for any other craft project.

MIXING CUPS

Small plastic mixing cups are handy for mixing enamel paints, but I also use them to hold small amounts of Klyr-Fire, as well as Scalex. I actually wear disposable contact lenses, so you can imagine what I use for my mixing cups. Small plastic medicine cups are also great too, but avoid using paper cups, as they can absorb the enamel paint **[13]**.

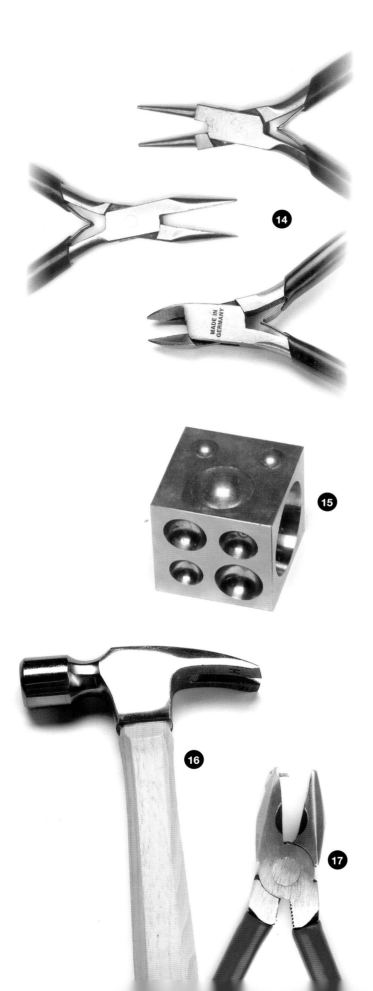

ROUNDNOSE PLIERS, CHAINNOSE PLIERS, AND WIRE CUTTERS

I have a very specific set of wire-wrapping tools for my enameling projects. They're a little down and dirty, because I take a rough-and-tumble approach to my designs. If you have high-quality wire-wrapping tools, they should be set aside and only used for stand-alone wire-wrapping. An affordable (economy-priced) set of tools can, quite literally, take the heat of working, with the enameling technique **[14]**.

DAPPING BLOCK AND PUNCH SET

This tool helps you give flat copper pieces a domed appearance. Good, affordable steel dapping block and punch sets can easily be found online. You'll find a variety of options available, but I own the most basic set and it gets the job done. Use it on a hard surface so the block stays stable and doesn't bounce **[15]**.

SMALL CLAW HAMMER

A hammer is a helpful tool to have in your enameling set up. You'll use it to flatten metal that might warp during the hole punching process. You also need one to help dome metal with the dapping block **[16]**.

HOLE-PUNCHING PLIERS

A hole punch is required for most, but not all of the projects. You might opt to use a more traditional screw-down helicopter punch, but also consider using hand-held, hole-punching pliers, which allow you to see exactly where you'll punch your metal. There are several sizes and versions on the market. I often use 1.25mm or 1.8mm hand-held hole punches. These pliers help avoid unintentional placement of holes, because you can see where you'll punch before you actually do so. They have replaceable punching pins too, so be sure to have extra pins on hand **[17]**.

⚠ SAFETY

I know I keep saying that torch enameling is all about playing–and it is.

But I have to get serious for just a moment to talk about safety. It's hugely important. We are heating glass and metal to 1400–1500 degrees Fahrenheit, after all. The good news is the following safety tips are all pretty straightforward. Being safe is mostly about using your head and letting common sense drive your decisions. Okay, here goes.

Choose a good workspace

You should work where you will be safe and comfortable. I am lucky to have a workshop space in my garage, which is where my torch enameling happens. The space you choose should be well-lit and well-ventilated. Indoors is probably best, as long as you have good ventilation. Torches and enamel will react to wind and rain and excessive heat and cold, so keep this in mind.

Your work area should include a sturdy table or counter to keep your kiln brick and trivet steady. It should be at a comfortable height for either sitting or standing (I'm more of a stander), and it should be large enough to hold your kiln brick, your enamels, the tools you are using, water bowls, and any reference materials you might want to have nearby.

Get to know your tools and materials

Your enamel, your torch, and other tools you will use will most likely come with instructions. Read them! I know may be the last thing you feel like doing, but you'll thank me later. Learning how to handle your tools and materials will keep you safe and keep your workspace in order. And it will likely inspire your creativity. Look for videos on YouTube and around the Web. Lots of companies offer great demo clips (such as beaducation. com!) and instructions for using their stuff.

Respect the hotness!

A good enameling torch can reach a temperature of about 2000 degrees. So yeah, it's hot. And so is the enamel, the copper, and the tools you will use in these projects. Please use caution. If you are worried about burns, you can always wear gloves. Confession: I rarely wear them, nor do I list gloves as a required tool, but as a beginner, you should considering wearing them, especially if it makes you more comfortable. Choose form-fitting leather or cloth gloves that won't limit your ability to work with smaller pieces and delicate enamel. I do keep a bowl of water nearby to keep my hands clean and for the occasional "owwie."

Enamel: Looks sweet, but do not eat!

It's super important to store your enamels somewhere safe. Make sure the lids are on tight and keep them out of the reach of small children and your pets. Enamels are very alluring and look like sugar or candy, but they are made from ground glass, kids! So it would not be nearly as fun as, say, eating paste. *Be very afraid.*

The same safety goes for your torches and gas. Store them in a cool, dry place out of direct sunlight. Butane gas tanks are under pressure, so treat them that way. Always make sure torches are properly turned off when you are done using them. And let them cool down before you put them away and close up shop.

Protect your soft assets

Just like in dodge ball or beauty pageants, it's important to protect your face, hands, and body when you torch enamel. Masks and safety glasses are a must. Fortunately, most enamels made today are lead-free (steer clear of leaded enamel), but it's still ground glass. Wear a mask to avoid ingesting or inhaling any of it, and work in a well-ventilated area. Be sure to wash your hands throughout the process to remove any loose enamel. I listed a few types of masks earlier, and safety glasses can be picked up at most hardware or craft stores.

Torch enameling is not a red carpet event. Wear very comfortable clothes, keep your hair out of harm's way, and avoid anything dangly or fringy that might interfere with your torch play. Similarly, don't wear a lot of jewelry while you're making jewelry. Or at least keep it simple. Safety first, fashionistas!

Keep it clean

As you become a frequent torch enameler, your workspace may start to get cluttered. It happens. Try and get into the habit of cleaning up a project area completely when it's done. That way, when you start something new, everything will be in its proper place and you won't have to put out an APB on your favorite enamel or tool.

Don't enamel under the influence

I know sometimes a few glasses of pinot can really get the creative juices flowing. But remember what I said about common sense? *Friends don't let friends operate torches while lit.* Enough said.

Okay, I'm taking off my fire-chief hat now. Be safe out there!

COOKIE SHEET

I like using metal cookie sheets as a work surface. They are easy to clean and transport around the house. Of course, my enameling cookie sheet is only for enameling and not for cookie baking! When I teach at larger shows, they often place galvanized steel sheets on the table. These sheets come in a variety of sizes and are easily found at larger hardware stores.

METAL SHEARS

Shears help make cutting metal a breeze. I use *Beaducation's* French shears. I discovered them a few years back and it was instant "amour." I love the compact size of these shears, as hardware store metal cutters or tin snips are often too bulky to maneuver tight corners. When using French shears, I cut from the edge of the metal toward the vertex (or corner) of angular shapes. This provides crisper lines, especially in tight corners **[18]**. I also anneal (heat) the copper before I cut it. When copper is heated and then cooled, it becomes more malleable and easier to cut. Keep in mind when you use shears, while it is a faster way to cut, it is a less precise option than a traditional jeweler's saw. However, if you've not used one before, the process can be frustrating. Cheers to shears!

PIPE CUTTER

This is one of those tools I never knew existed until I wanted to work with copper pipe. It is a specialized tool found at larger hardware stores. I prefer the adjustable version, which allows you to work with different pipe diameters. Simply place the pipe inside the tool, so it rests on the wheels. Next, adjust the tool, so the blade makes contact with the pipe. Avoid over-tightening the tool, as you'll dent the pipe. Twist the pipe to make the first score line, then twist again. The tool will need to be gently tightened as you continue to rotate the pipe. You'll also notice the score line is getting deeper and deeper until it eventually

cuts through completely. The blades do dull over time, but you can purchase replacements. You can use a jeweler's saw to cut through the pipe, but I find the pipe cutter to be fast and easy to use **[19]**.

GLASS BOWLS OR SAUCERS

Whenever I work with in-flame enameling and need to immerse hot copper or wire into enamel, I pour a generous amount of enamel into a small glass tea-light holder or onto a small glass saucer. You might consider setting aside enamel to be used exclusively for in-flame enameling **[20]**.

BUTANE GAS

A multi-refined butane gas helps keep your torch working correctly. While these types of gases are a bit more expensive than others, I prefer them over basic butane gas. The flame is cleaner and appropriate for work with in-flame enameling versus firing directly onto the triveted project. I have two go-to gases: Blazer Butane and Vector Butane (the latter is available at Williams-Sonoma).

C-CLAMPS

Small c-clamps help hold torches and their bases in place. The Max Flame torch comes with a small, black, plastic base. I've taken to clamping this base into place so the torch is more stable. A small lip protrudes from the plastic base and should be in back of the torch. The longer protrusion is what you will clamp to. You can spend some time building a permanent base, by screwing the plastic base to a large piece of wood. As most projects require you to hold the torch directly, this firing process is relatively safe. but with some projects, it is best if the torch is stationary. A clamped torch allows you the flexibility to work with two hands during the enameling process. (Do NOT let go of the lit torch if the base is not secured!)

RIVETING TOOL

There are a few types of riveting tools on the market and I've used the more affordable version: the EZ Riveting System by Beadsmith. The riveting tool is a two-part system. One part of the tool punches a specific-sized hole, while the other part of the tool is used for riveting. You must use very specific rivets with this system. The rivets come in a variety of lengths, metals, and colors.

ENAMELS

Vitreous enamels come in so many colors. Most designers I know get their enamels from Thompson Enamels. I often encourage beginners to work with opaque enamels first, but transparent enamels also have an appeal as well. I use transparent enamels with fine silver because I love how these two materials work together. Typically when you order enamels, they are ground and good to go. For all of the projects here, you're using medium expansion enamels for copper. The flow point for enamels is as varied as the colors, but for the most part, the enamels will begin to do their thing around 1400–1500 degrees Fahrenheit [21].

ENAMEL PAINTS

I love enamel paint! These are also sold by Thompson Enamels. What makes them so amazing is that you can easily blend them to create new colors. The customization these enamel paints can provide to a designer is incredible. They are sold in tubes and look like acrylic paint, but can be fired in the same way as traditional powder enamel. Working with enamel paints can be a little tricky at first. Because you are often dealing with small amounts of paint, recognizing the firing stages can be a little more difficult than with powdered enamel. But the end result—a glossy finish—is the same [22].

SMALL WASH CLOTHS

These are handy for clean up. Avoid cheap cloths that shed fibers, as they can sometimes stick to the copper and become trapped in the enamel as you sift, only to reappear during the firing process. And when they show up—so do the cracks.

MICA

You'll use the sheet form of this natural mineral. It can withstand the high heat of the torch flame and is perfect as a backing for hollow projects, such as tubes. Often sold in large 4x4-in. sheets, it can be easily cut down to the size you'll need. Small pieces of mica will often stick to the back of a project, but can be easily removed with a diamond file [23].

ETCHING CREAM

This cream is a fast and easy way to create a faux-sandblasted, matte finish on glass. While a handy tool to have, it is extremely caustic, so it is important to wear rubber gloves as you work with this product. After the cream is applied, it only takes 5–7 minutes to etch. It can be used in various ways across entire surfaces, or, using a stencil, you can add a matte finish to individual parts of your piece.

VERMICULITE

A small bowl of vermiculite is a great way to slowly and gently cool projects that might not withstand an environment with unstable air temperatures. I often place my wire and three-dimensional (curved/sculptural) pieces in vermiculite and leave the two-dimensional (flat) pieces on the kiln brick to cool. I also place the vermiculite on a small mug warmer as well. Small bags of vermiculite can easily be found online.

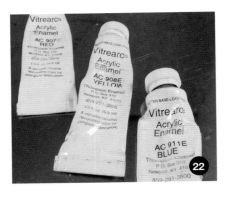

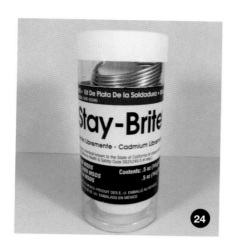

SOLDER

I first learned to solder using the following products. If you've used other products, that's fine. Just bear in mind, the solder melting point should be lower than the fuse temperature of your enamel. If the solder melting temperature is too close to the fuse temperature of the enamel, you risk overfiring the enamel as well. The following two solders I recommend have melting temperatures far below that of the enameling fuse temperature.

STAY-BRITE (COIL SOLDER)

Use this to solder most metal AFTER you've enameled your project pieces. With a melting temperature of 430 degrees F, you'll be able to create connections without harming the enamel. However, your torch flame should always be significantly shorter and smaller than what you would use for enameling. Stay-Brite is sold as a coil, but you can quickly flatten small pieces to use as chips **[24]**.

SOLDER-IT (COPPER BEARING PASTE)

This is a soft solder widely available at larger hardware stores. It has a low melting point and therefore can be used with projects that are already enameled. The product is sold as a syringe, with the solder and flux are combined to make it easier to use. I've often told students it is a down-and-dirty approach to soldering and to use this product only if the metal will hide the solder. This product is most often used by plumbers who are working to repair copper pipe and are typically less concerned with the aesthetics of the solder. If you're a designer interested in working with a different type of solder, be mindful that a higher-temperature solder will take more heat and potentially damage your enamel.

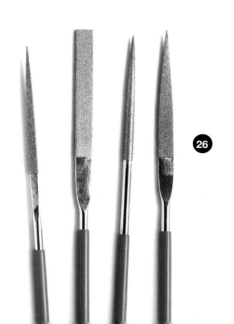

METAL FILES

A small collection of various sized metal files can help smooth out rough spots on the copper, especially burrs occurring when holes are punched (especially when using dull hole punches). I use a variety of files, depending on the size of the copper. Hand files are perfect tools to have at the table. You'll also need metal files to help finish off edges cut with the French shears. Emery boards can help shine up and remove the oxidization of the edges from the copper **[25]**.

DIAMOND FILES

A decent diamond file is a must-have tool when working with enamel. Big or small, these tools help remove fired enamel from the sides of your projects. Bear in mind the diamond file will leave a matte finish on any enamel it comes in contact with, so be specific and intentional about the area you're trying to clean up. I use a smaller set for smaller pieces and tight corners, and larger files for big jobs, like removing glass burrs from the backside of a project **[26]**.

ENAMELING 101

Before we dive into specific projects, I want to give you a basic understanding of the steps of a typical enameling process. Instructions will vary from project to project, but this should give you a general understanding of how enameling works.

WHAT IS ENAMELING?

In simple terms, enameling is the art of using heat to apply glass (vitreous enamels) to a metal surface, such as copper. There are two ways to enamel: using a torch and using a kiln. This book is all about the torch.

YOUR MAIN TOOLS AND MATERIALS

These will vary by project, but here's what most require:
- Copper (flat pieces, pipe, and wire)
- Opaque, transparent, and paint enamels
- High-quality butane torch and butane, stainless steel trivets, and a quality kiln brick
- Small enameling sifter
- Old magazines
- Penny Brite, small wash cloth, old toothbrush, water
- Protective equipment: dust mask and safety glasses or goggles
- Finishing equipment: standard metal and diamond files

CLEANING YOUR COPPER: A LITTLE WORK—THEN LOTS OF FUN

All copper should be punched and cleaned before you work with it. There are exceptions to this rule, which you'll see in some of the projects. But the secret weapon for me is Penny Brite. It makes the cleaning process so much easier.

CREATING AN ENAMELING STATION AND FIRING STATION:

Don't worry. This can all happen in the same general work area, but it's a good idea to have a clean surface where you are applying enamel powder. This specific are should be separate from your firing area, which will consist of your kiln brick, stainless-steel trivet or titanium pick, and torch.

COUNTERENAMELING: DO IT FIRST

Counterenameling is done to the backside of your piece and consists of one to two coats of enamel. Counterenameling stabilizes the piece and prevents the front from chipping, cracking, and coming apart from the front of the copper. Counterenameling should be the first step in the enameling process. Using black or another neutral color makes the process much easier. Torch firing can potentially alter the appearance of the counterenamel. Therefore, I always recommend using black and avoid designing on the backside of the piece.

FIRING YOUR PROJECT

You hold the power in your hands. Literally! As you know, this technique involves extremely hot temperatures, so always be aware of your surroundings. Ensure your firing station (kiln brick and trivet) are stable and all combustible materials have been removed from the area.

WORKING UNDER, OVER, AND IN IT!

When powdered enamel comes into direct contact with the torch flame, it will heat up and may char quickly, so the best approach is to fire from underneath your project. As I mentioned earlier, there are exceptions to this rule and you'll see

Adding enamel to your pieces:

To apply the enamel, you will use a mesh screen sifter. You will apply an even coat to your project, sifting from a starting point, and following the shape of the piece. The key to applying the enamel is to do so as evenly as possible.

Once the copper piece has been coated, carefully place it onto your firing trivet or titanium pick. There are a variety of ways to transfer projects from the sifting surface to the trivet. You can use a pair of fine-point tweezers or you can sift onto a short plastic bottle, with the metal slightly over the edge of the cap. This method allows you to easily pick up the metal and transfer to the trivet, but be mindful if you've just fired on the trivet – it will be hot! At times I also hold the copper on my finger and sift away—it can be quite messy and you MUST rinse your finger as soon as you've transferred the project. However, when working with curved pieces, this may help you tilt the copper to get even coverage.

Stages of the firing process in traditional enameling:

First stage: Sugar. As the enamel melts, the powder begins to form small granules, similar to sugar **[1]**.

Second stage: Orange Peel. As the enamel continues to melt, it takes on the appearance and texture of an orange peel **[2, 3]**.

Final stage: Fully Fused. When enamel is properly fired, the surface should appear glossy and smooth **[4]**.

Overdid-it stage: Over-fired. If a piece is over-fired, a few things can happen. The enamel can pull away from the edge, exposing the copper, which produces firescale, which can in turn jump into the enamel and become a permanent part of your piece. The enamel can also begin to break down and form pits throughout the piece. When working with wire, it is easy to over-fire enamel, as the enamel will want to flow up the wire and the wire will want to work its way out. So be mindful of the amount of time your wire is in the flame.

them in some of the projects. Remember to always angle your torch up toward the project at a 45-degree angle or so, as opposed to holding it straight up at 90 degrees. When firing on the trivet, keep the flame off the front of the piece, as it can scorch the enamel.

I also encourage students to use the residual heat from the kiln brick to help with the process. You might consider rotating the brick around, so you can send heat back up towards the project. In that instance, you're firing at 45-degree angle down toward the brick. Your flame is about 2½–3 in. long, so be sure your hand isn't directly over the brick. I find the cleanest

part of the butane flame to be at the far end, about 1½ in. from the end of the blue flame. When working with wire, you can avoid scorching your project by staying in that section of the flame.

COOLING AND CLEANING

Once the project cools, copper not covered by enamel will be covered in firescale. This oxidization needs to be removed before any more enamel is applied to the surface. Do not quench hot projects in water, as it will thermally shock the glass. Allow hot pieces to gradually cool on their own or place them in vermiculite to slowly cool them.

A resource on the Interweb!

The torch-firing technique requires patience and practice, and of course, safety should always be at the forefront of your mind. If you've never watched my basic torch-enameling video, put a book-mark on this page and head over to **macaroniandglitter. com/videos**. It is an awesome companion piece to this book and a helpful resource you can watch as many times as you need!

Your Coefficient of Expansion... say what?

Sorry to get all scientific here, but as a beginner, the COE is something to think about as you develop your skills. (It's also fun to drop on people at cocktail parties.) Simply put, COE is an equation associated with how your glass melts (or softens) and expands, as well as its fit with the metal you're using. There are various fusion flow points, the speed and the temperature at which glass flows. The enamels I suggest using for these projects (medium expansion enamels) have a COE between 258-360. The softening point at which the glass will begin to flow is between 1400 and 1500 degrees. Within a single project, it's important to use enamels with compatible COEs. If the COEs are too varied, you can run into problems of either overfiring or underfiring the enamel. Okay, science lesson over.

Beyond The Basics

EMBEDDED METAL COMIC BOOK
EARRINGS

I've always been drawn to the bold colors and larger-than-life imagery of the comic book motif. These earrings are made even more fun with the addition of enameled letters. Most people would say earrings are supposed to match, so to avoid an international incident, use the same colors on both sides. But a different word on each ear sounds way more fun to me!

YOU'LL NEED

- Copper letters (beaducation.com)
- 3x3 in. 22-gauge copper sheet
- 2–4 7mm jump rings
- Pair of earring wires
- Permanent marker
- Transparent enamel (Egg Yellow)
- Black counterenamel (I used 1995.)
- Opaque enamels (Titanium White and Darkest Blue)
- French shears

- Mesh screen
- Penny Brite, old toothbrush, and small towel
- Kiln brick, trivet, fine-point tweezers, torch, and titanium pick
- Sifter, dust mask, and magazine sheets
- Hole-punching pliers and metal file
- Bentnose pliers
- Small claw hammer and bench block

PREPARE THE METAL

I prefer to cut out my "star" design directly from the copper sheet. The thinner gauge makes it much easier to use the French shears. First, draw your design onto the copper sheet with a permanent marker. (You can trace it on a piece of cardstock.)

Next, use the shears to cut out the individual pieces **[1]**. Cut one line at a time, in one direction, and try to always begin your cuts from an open edge versus a tight angle. This will result in cleaner cuts and help minimize bending of the metal. Repeat the process for the other star, and then punch a hole near the top edge of each star. Use a hammer and bench block to flatten the star **[2]**.

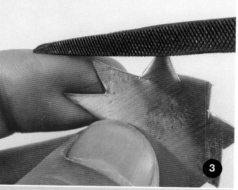

Prepare the stars as in "Cleaning Your Copper," p. 16. File down any sharp points or burrs **[3]**.

COUNTERENAMEL

Counterenamel the backside of both pieces **[4]**. Fire the counterenamel, allow it to cool, and then clean the front of each star. Set these two pieces aside.

> ### NOTE
> For this project, I used a base coat of **Titanium White**, **Darkest Blue** for the letters, and a splash of transparent **Egg Yellow**. You can also try bright primary-colored enamels, such as **Orient Red**, **Marigold Yellow**, **Ultramarine Blue**, and **Hunter Green**.

Enamel the Letters

This is one of the few times I don't counterenamel the back side of the copper. Clean and dry the letters and then place them on a mesh screen. Carefully sift the enamel on the copper **[5]**, and then fire from underneath the letters **[6]**. Remove from the screen, allow the letters to cool, and then thoroughly remove the firescale from the back and sides of the letters.

NOTE

The letters are tiny, so there isn't a great way to transfer them after sifting. I used this particular mesh screen exclusively for firing these letters. If you try and re-use the screen, keep in mind that residual enamel from the sifting process may stick to future projects.

PUT THE PIECES TOGETHER

Once all of the metal pieces are cleaned, you're ready to fire the letters directly into the enamel on the front side of the starburst. Select a contrasting color (or colors) and sift onto the front of the star **[7]**. The letters need to settle into the enamel while you fire, so you need a more-than-normal amount of enamel on the front. Using a pair of fine-point tweezers, carefully drop the letters into the unfired enamel and use a titanium pick to adjust their positions, if necessary **[8]**. Using the pick, lightly push all of the letters into place so the edges of the letters are all surrounded by enamel. Fire the full piece on your trivet until the bottom layer of enamel is set **[9]**.

Allow the piece to cool, remove it from the trivet, and then clean the edges of each star.

FINISH THE EARRINGS

Connect each star to an earring wire with a jump ring or two.

 TRY SOMETHING DIFFERENT

You can enamel smaller pieces of copper and layer them into a larger piece. See my website, macaroniandglitter.com, for photos of pieces inspired by these projects.

SCRATCH ART
PENDANTS

This is my twist on the sgraffito (scratching) technique. It was one of the first techniques I taught to students. Do you remember those iconic sheets of scratch art paper? They were covered in a black wax and with just a few scratches here and there, you could reveal a rainbow of colors. The beauty of this project is you can create intricate designs or simple freeform styles with random scratching.

YOU'LL NEED

- 5 25.4x6.4mm copper rectangles
- 18–20 in. (46–51cm) fancy chain
- 7 6mm jump rings
- Lobster claw clasp
- Black counterenamel (I used 1995; this is also the base for the front.)
- 4 or more opaque enamels in bright primary colors, such as Orient Red, Marigold Yellow, Ultramarine Blue, and Hunter Green
- Black enamel paint

- Small paintbrush
- Scratching tool with a sharp point
- Water for painting and cleaning
- Penny Brite, old toothbrush, and small towel
- Kiln brick, trivet, torch, bentnose pliers, tweezers, and titanium pick
- Sifter, dust mask, and magazine sheets
- Hole-punching pliers

PREPARE THE METAL

Prepare the two copper rectangles as in "Cleaning Your Copper," p. 16. Punch a hole at the top of each rectangle.

COUNTERENAMEL

Counterenamel the back side of the piece with the black enamel. (You'll add a thin layer to the front side of the piece later, so keep the materials nearby for that step.) Fire the counterenamel, allow it to cool, and then clean the front of each rectangle.

ENAMEL

Add a thin layer of black enamel to the front of each rectangle and fire it **[1]**. Once it's cool, add your opaque background colors (I prefer to fire them separately.) Start with red **[2]**, fire, and then allow the rectangle to cool. Next, apply the yellow **[3]**. Use the small paintbrush to create a distinct line between colors **[4]**. Fire again. Repeat until all colors have been fired on the front, making sure you have an even level of colors **[5]**.

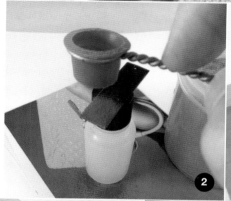

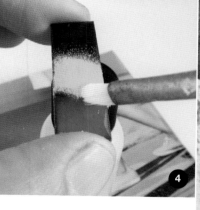

PAINT

Now apply a layer of black enamel paint over the entire design—a few drops of water will help thin the paint, which should completely black out the colors **[6]**. You might need to continually dab the piece to cover the background colors. Allow the enamel paint to dry, completely.

SCRATCH

Next, take the scratching tool and create your design **[7]**. (If the paint flakes off in small chunks, it was too thin. You can simply wash off the black paint and start again.) Once you have the desired design, fully fire the piece **[8]**. Before you fire, you'll notice the paint has a chalky appearance; it is fully fired once it has become glossy. Allow it to cool and then clean edges.

FINISH THE NECKLACE

Make five pendants. Cut a piece of fancy chain to the desired length. (My necklace is made with bar-and-loop chain.) Attach a jump ring to one end, and use a jump ring to attach a lobster claw clasp on the other end. Attach each pendant to a link of chain with a jump ring, spacing them as desired.

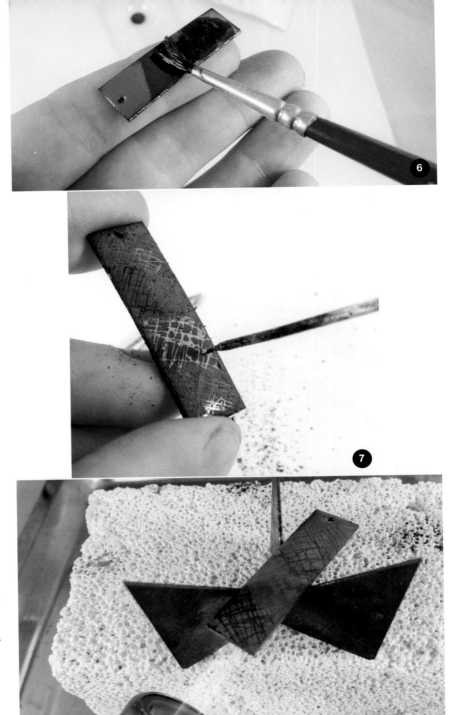

 TRY SOMETHING DIFFERENT

I used black enamel paint because I wanted to mimic the look of traditional scratch art paper, but you might also consider changing the background colors and using a different enamel paint color. Keep it high-contrast or make it monochromatic for a variety of vibrant designs.

SUGAR SKULLS
PENDANTS

I live in a city that loves to celebrate *Dia de los Muertos* (Day of the Dead). It is such a beautiful celebration and I love all of the traditions associated with this holiday. I've made real sugar skulls, but decided it was time to re-create them with enamel. The three-dimensional aspect of this piece makes it very appealing to designers. If you don't have a dapping block, consider keeping the piece flat—it will still be bold and beautiful!

YOU'LL NEED

- 1-in. (2.5cm) copper disk
- 4 10mm metal connectors
- 21 in. (53cm) rosary chain
- 10 jump rings in different sizes
- Black counterenamel (I used 1995.)
- Titanium White enamel
- A selection of primary enameling paint colors (Remember, you can blend the colors to create specialized colors.)
- Klyr-Fire

- French shears
- Several small paintbrushes and permanent marker
- Titanium pick or other sharp scratching tool
- Penny Brite, old toothbrush, and small towel
- Kiln brick, trivet, torch, bentnose pliers, and fine-point tweezers
- Sifter, dust mask, and magazine sheets
- Hole-punching pliers
- Steel dapping block
- Small claw hammer and bench block
- Metal files
- 2 pairs of chainnose pliers
- Wire cutters

PREPARE THE METAL

You'll need to cut and shape the metal before you enamel. First anneal the copper, so it is easier to cut and dome. Place it on the kiln brick and heat it until it glows a soft, rosy red. Let the metal cool, then draw a skull shape onto it **[1]**.

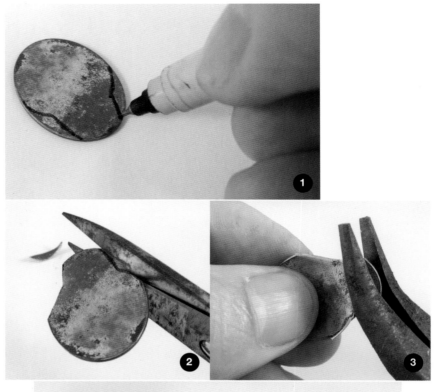

Use French shears to remove the sides of the jawbone **[2]**. Save them for a scrap project or discard. Next, you'll dome the top part of the skull—don't worry about the jawbone, as you will flatten it later. Place the copper in a dapping block and shape. Anneal the piece one more time, let it cool, and then place the jawbone between the jaws of bentnose pliers to flatten and bend it **[3]**. Place the skull on a steel bench block and use a small hammer to flatten the jawbone.

COUNTERENAMEL

Prepare the skull component as described in "Cleaning Your Copper," p. 16. Punch a hole near the top. Next, counterenamel the back side of the skull component with black enamel: Paint a thin coat of Klyr-Fire on the skull component **[4]** and sift on the black counterenamel. Fire the counterenamel and allow it to cool.

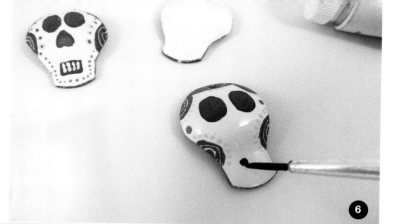

ENAMEL

Clean the front of the skull component. Apply a thin coat of Klyr-Fire, then sift a layer of white enamel **[5]** and fire.

ADD THE DESIGN

Once the skull component is cool, you can begin to add your design with enamel paints **[6, 7]**. You'll find a variety of calavera (skull) designs on the Internet (make sure they are copyright-free) or you can use some of the designs on this page to inspire you. Apply the enamel paint directly to the surface, and if desired, allow to dry and then scratch in designs. It's helpful to allow the enamel paint to dry before adding new colors, as this will help you avoid unintentional blending. This project provides endless design possibilities, so get creative!

Once you've completed painting your design, fully fire the piece. Before you fire, you'll notice the enamel paint has a chalky appearance—it is fully fired once it is glossy **[8]**. Allow it to cool and then clean the edges as desired.

FINISH THE NECKLACE

Cut two 2-in. (5cm) and two 5-in. (13cm) pieces of rosary chain. Connect a jump ring to the skull component. Then use a jump ring to connect the skull component and two pieces of rosary chain. On each end, connect a metal connector with a jump ring and then connect another strand of rosary chain to the other side of the connector with a jump ring. Attach another connector with jump rings. Connect a 9-in. (23cm) piece of rosary chain to each connector with a jump ring.

 TRY SOMETHING DIFFERENT

Experiment with different sizes of copper. Larger pieces of copper might require the use of a larger torch and smaller pieces of copper are perfect for a pair of earrings. As this project allows you to use a variety of designs, don't worry about matching the earrings—it is far more festive to have two different skulls!

WORKING WITH WASHERS NECKLACE

Students love working with washers, but they soon discover these shapes aren't the best pieces of metal to enamel. Often, they end up with burned, blackened enamel on the front of their project. So what's the secret to success? The key to working with washers is to use indirect heat reflected up from the kiln brick. This heat will fuse the glass to the metal without the tip of the flame shooting through the washer and ultimately discoloring the enamel on the front.

YOU'LL NEED

- 6 18-gauge copper washer shapes ranging from 14.25–20.7mm
- 6 6mm jump rings
- Assorted seed beads
- Bar half of a toggle clasp
- Beading wire
- 2 crimp beads
- Black counterenamel (I used 1995.)
- Opaque enamels (A collection from the same color family makes the project pop.)

- Permanent marker
- Penny Brite, old toothbrush, and small towel
- Kiln brick, trivet, torch, bentnose pliers, titanium pick, and fine-point tweezers
- Sifter, dust mask, and magazine sheets
- Hole-punching pliers
- Wire cutters and diamond file
- 2 pairs of chainnose pliers and crimping pliers
- Wire cutters

PREPARE THE METAL

Some students opt to use washers without punching a hole in them. They do, after all, have a huge hole right in the center. But for this design, you'll need holes on both sides of the washers. Prepare the washers as described in "Cleaning Your Copper," p. 16. Use a permanent marker to mark where you will make the holes and use hole-punching pliers or a screw-down punch to create the holes (Make a smaller-sized hole, about 1.25mm, as the width of the metal is often pretty narrow.) **[1]**.

COUNTERENAMEL

Clean the washer and then sift black counterenamel on the back side. Transfer **[2]** the metal to the trivet. Firing washers is very different from firing other pieces of metal because you'll point your torch flame towards the kiln brick rather than the metal, so that heat rises from the brick and ultimately flows the enamel **[3]**. I often rotate the brick, so I can point the flame at different angles.

Continue firing until the surface is glossy and smooth—remember, the kiln brick will be very hot! Remove the metal, allow it to cool, and then clean the firescale off of the front side.

ENAMEL

When you are ready to add color to the front, repeat the sifting process **[4]**. Clear the enamel from the holes with a pick. If you don't have a hole, simply grab the metal from the sides. Transfer your piece to the trivet and repeat the firing steps **[5, 6, 7, 8]**. Allow it to cool and remove from the trivet. Remove the excess enamel and firescale from the sides of your piece with a diamond file, then rinse and dry the piece.

FINISH THE NECKLACE

Make five washers punched with two holes and one washer punched with one hole as shown in the project photo on p. 30. Connect the washers in a row with jump rings. On one end, you'll have a free jump ring: String a crimp bead on a piece of beading wire and crimp the crimp bead to the jump ring. String a pattern of seed beads in different sizes and shapes, and then crimp the bar half of a toggle clasp on the other end of the beading wire. Clasp the necklace by inserting the bar through one of the washers.

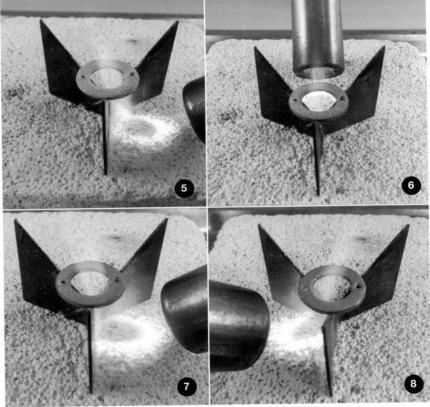

 TRY SOMETHING DIFFERENT

Candy—Olympic rings—donuts. With all their different shapes and sizes, washers can inspire many iconic objects and designs. It seems like the more color, and the more washers, the better. Go big!

CONFETTI
EARRINGS

This is my ode to Jackson Pollock, the artist famous in part for his drip paintings. I was so excited to discover enamel paints, because they really are a fantastic medium for creating truly custom projects.

PREPARE THE METAL

Use a permanent marker to mark where you will punch the holes. (Mark one hole at the top of the disk, and mark five holes evenly spaced along the bottom.) Use hole-punching pliers to make the holes on both disks.

Prepare the disks as in "Cleaning Your Copper," p. 16. File down any sharp points or burrs.

NOTE

When a project has several holes, the Penny Brite can get caught and block the holes. Use a pick to make sure the holes are clear before adding counternamel.

COUNTERENAMEL

Counterenamel the back side of both pieces with the black enamel. Fire counterenamel, allow to cool, and then clean the front.

ENAMEL

Add the background color to the front of the disks (in this case, Titanium White) **[1]**. Fire and let cool. Pick up disk by the edges **[2]** and move to the trivet for firing **[3]**. Remove any firescale from the edges of both disks.

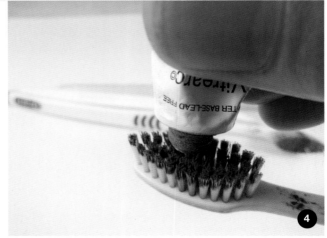

ADD THE PAINT SPLATTERS

Lay both disks on a sheet of paper, front side facing up. Add a small amount of enamel paint to the tooth-brush and rub it into the bristles **[4]**—you won't need much. Next, holding the brush head over the metal, gently flick the bristles, creating small splatters on the surface of the disks.

Continue this process, switching out paint colors, until you have used all three colors and you are satisfied with the coverage. Use a pair of fine-point tweezers to transfer the metal pieces to a trivet **[5]** and fire the pieces until the paint is glossy like the background **[6]**. Allow to cool and if desired, add additional splatters and fire again.

FINISH THE EARRINGS

On each headpin, string a small seed bead, a larger seed bead, another small seed bead, and make a plain loop. Connect each seed-bead dangle to one of the holes on the bottom of the disk **[7]**. Attach an earring wire to the top hole in each disk with a jump ring. Repeat to make a second earring.

 TRY SOMETHING DIFFERENT

For this project, I used Titanium White as my background. It is my favorite white, because it is incredibly bright. However, feel free to play around with background colors and find the design that's all you. For best results, I recommend using contrasting colors between the background colors and the paint splatter colors.

Fantastic Finishes

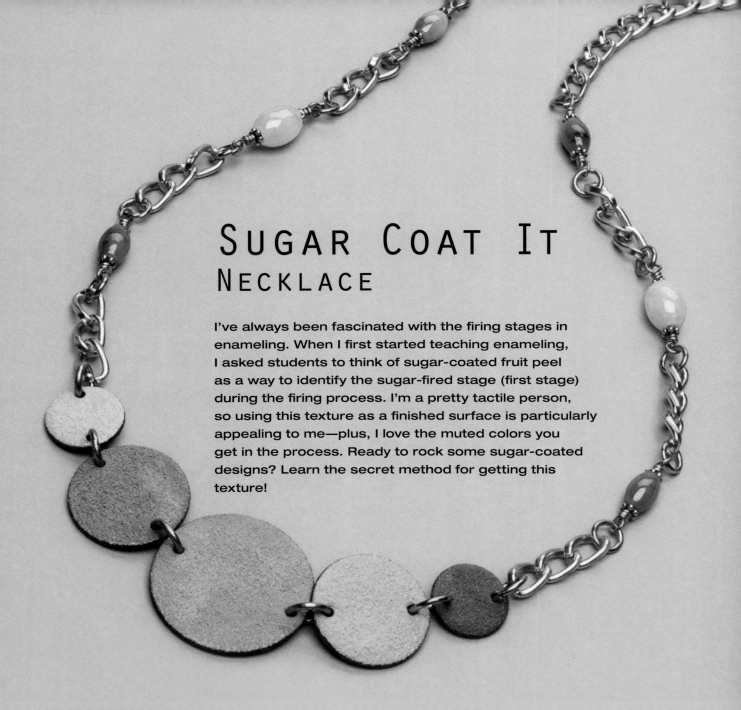

Sugar Coat It
Necklace

I've always been fascinated with the firing stages in enameling. When I first started teaching enameling, I asked students to think of sugar-coated fruit peel as a way to identify the sugar-fired stage (first stage) during the firing process. I'm a pretty tactile person, so using this texture as a finished surface is particularly appealing to me—plus, I love the muted colors you get in the process. Ready to rock some sugar-coated designs? Learn the secret method for getting this texture!

You'll need

- 5 18-gauge copper disks in a variety of diameters
- 6 4–8mm oval beads
- 12 bead spacers
- 19–20 6–7mm jump rings
- 20 in. (51cm) chain
- 6 3-in. (7.6mm) headpins
- Lobster claw clasp
- Opaque enamels (I find a collection from the same color family makes the project pop.)
- Black counterenamel (I used 1995.)
- Permanent marker
- Penny Brite, old toothbrush, and small towel
- Kiln brick, trivet, torch, bentnose pliers, and tweezers
- Sifter, dust mask, and magazine sheets
- Hole-punching pliers
- Chainnose pliers and roundnose pliers
- Wire cutters

COUNTERENAMEL

Follow the steps to make as many blanks as you need for the necklace (mine has five).

Punch a single hole in the disk. To ensure your second hole is directly opposite the first one, draw a line from one side to the other. Punch the second hole. Prepare the disk as in "Cleaning Your Copper," p. 16. Next, add the counterenamel to the backside of the piece, fire it, and then allow it to cool **[1, 2]**. To speed up the process, counterenamel all of the pieces you're creating at once, allowing them to cool on the side of the kiln brick.

ENAMEL

Clean the front side of the metal. Once it's dry, you're ready to add your first layer of enamel to the front. Select your color and sift it onto the metal. Fire the piece until the enamel has gone through all stages and is glossy and smooth. Once it's cooled off, add another layer of the same color to the metal. This time when you fire it, you'll want to stop when the enamel reaches the sugar coat stage. Closely monitor the changes in the enamel—with smaller pieces of metal, it can be easy to overfire the enamel and move beyond the sugar coat stage into the orange peel stage **[3, 4, 5]**. Remember, you must always have at least one layer of fully-fired enamel under any semi-fired sugar coat layer. Single layers of sugar-coat texture not stabilized by a fully-fused enamel undercoat will break off of the metal. Once the sugar-fired layer has cooled, remove your piece from the trivet and carefully clean the edges.

Finish the Necklace

Make five disks of various sizes and connect them with jump rings [6]. Make six bead links using the headpins, oval beads, and spacers (string a spacer on each side of the bead). Cut the chain into six three-link pieces. On each side, connect a piece of chain to the end disk with a jump ring. Using jump rings, connect a bead link, a piece of chain, a bead link, a piece of chain, and a bead link to each end. Connect a 10-link piece of chain to each end. Connect a clasp at one end with a jump ring.

These pieces can be pulled into a variety of jewelry designs, but with their intriguing texture, I think they make great stand-alone pendants. Keep in mind that you'll yield different results with different opaque colors, so explore away!

 TRY SOMETHING DIFFERENT

Once you master this technique, you can experiment with the sugar-coat texture and add it to a small portion of a design. You'll still need to add the sugar-coat texture to a fully-fused glass surface, but block a section of the fused enamel with a small piece of paper as you sift. Alternatively, you can use a small paintbrush to remove the unfired enamel before you fire.

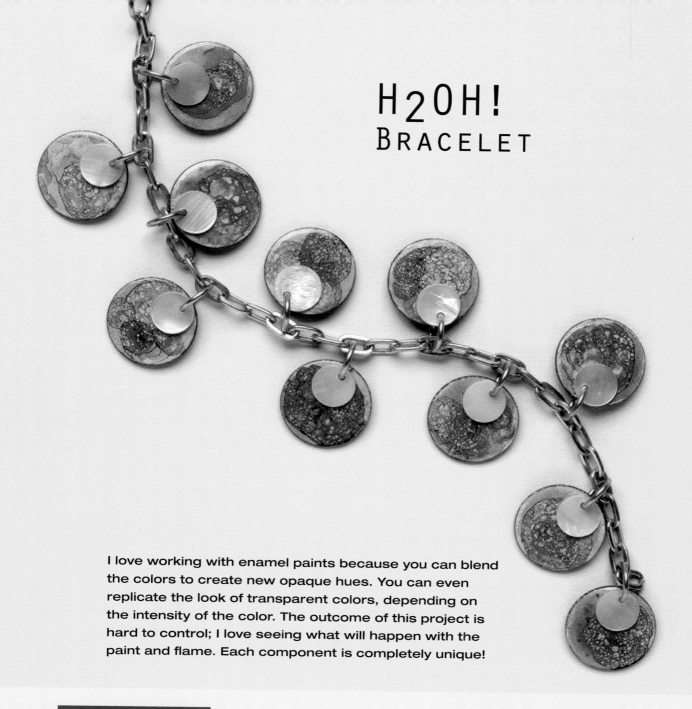

H₂OH!
BRACELET

I love working with enamel paints because you can blend the colors to create new opaque hues. You can even replicate the look of transparent colors, depending on the intensity of the color. The outcome of this project is hard to control; I love seeing what will happen with the paint and flame. Each component is completely unique!

YOU'LL NEED

- 11 25.4mm 18-gauge copper disks
- 11 8–10mm mother-of-pearl disk beads
- 8 in. (20cm) chain
- 12 8mm jump rings
- Lobster claw clasp
- Light background color (I used Titanium White.)
- Black counterenamel (I used 1995.)
- Enamel paints (I used Basic Blue.)

- Small paintbrush and water for painting
- Penny Brite, old toothbrush, and small towel
- Kiln brick, trivet, torch, bentnose pliers, and fine-point tweezers
- Sifter, dust mask, and magazine sheets
- Hole-punching pliers
- 2 pairs of chainnose pliers

ENAMEL

Follow the steps to make as many blanks as you need for the bracelet (mine has 11).

Use hole-punching pliers to create a hole in the copper disk. Prepare the disk as in "Cleaning Your Copper," p. 16. Once it's dry, add counterenamel to the back of the disk. Use fine-point tweezers to carefully place the disk on your firing trivet.

Fire the counterenamel and allow it to cool for approximately 5–10 minutes before removing the firescale with Penny Brite.

Once the firescale is removed from the front of the project, add the background color; light colors allow the top layer of enamel paints to be seen more clearly, so I used white enamel. Using colors too similar will result in the loss of the design. Fire the enamel and allow it to cool.

CREATE THE BUBBLES

Getting the bubble effect is easy, but it requires a watery solution of enamel paint. Work on the trivet directly to complete the design. Use a paint-brush to add a layer of enamel paint **[1]**. Then add a few drops of water and mix it in with the paint **[2]**. Slowly introduce the flame from below **[3]**. As the water evaporates, the bubble effect will form **[4]**.

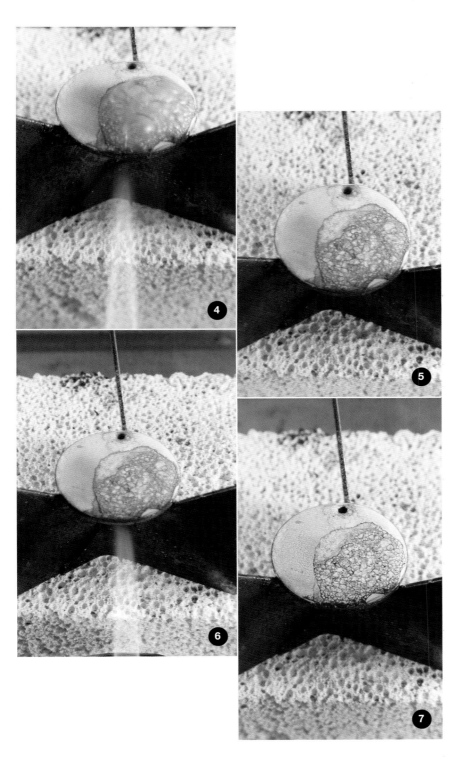

Add more water and enamel paint as needed. DO NOT fully fire the project until you get the desired bubble effect. If you don't like the look of the bubbles, wait a few minutes, then add a few more drops of water to reactivate the paint. Or add a bit more paint if needed and reintroduce the heat **[5, 6]**.

Once you have the desired bubbling effect, fully fire the project until the paints have gone from a chalky to a glassy appearance **[7]**. Allow the disk to cool before removing from the trivet.

FINISH THE BRACELET

Use jump rings to connect the copper disks and mother-of-pearl disk beads to the chain, skipping two links between disks. Attach a lobster claw clasp half to one end of the chain with a jump ring.

 ## TRY SOMETHING DIFFERENT

Don't want the bubble effect? Some designers love the look of the "tissue paper" or what I describe as the "Georgia O'Keefe" look. To achieve this, avoid boiling the water, but rather apply indirect heat to the trivet. The water will evaporate more slowly and this will minimize the appearance of bubbles. You can also allow your project to air dry before firing.

SALTED ENAMEL
BRACELET

If you've worked with watercolors before, you may remember the trick of using salt to absorb and ultimately draw the watercolors to a specific area of a painting. This technique incorporates that concept, but when the project is fired with the salt, it leaves behind an intriguing texture.

YOU'LL NEED

- 5 18-gauge copper blanks (I used 20.5mm rounded squares and a 25x18mm oval.)
- 4 6mm round gemstone beads
- 2 5–6mm jump rings
- 8 in. (20cm) 20-gauge craft wire
- Lobster claw clasp
- Black counterenamel (I used 1020.)
- Background enamel color (I used Titanium White.)
- Enamel paints and containers

- Table salt
- Small paintbrush and water
- Penny Brite, old toothbrush, and small towel
- Kiln brick, trivet, torch, bentnose pliers, and fine-point tweezers
- Sifter, dust mask, and magazine sheets
- 2mm hole-punching pliers
- Roundnose pliers and chainnose pliers
- Wire cutters

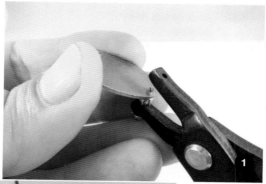

PREPARE THE BLANKS

Follow the steps to make as many blanks as you need for the bracelet (mine has five).

Use hole-punching pliers to punch a hole close to the edge of a metal blank **[1]**. Make another hole on the other side of the blank.

Prepare the blank as in "Cleaning Your Copper," p. 16. Once dry, add counterenamel to the back of the blank **[2]**. When the blank is coated, use fine-point tweezers to carefully place it on a firing trivet.

FIRE THE METAL

Fire the blank and allow it to cool. Remove the firescale with copper cleaner. Add the background color to the front of the component. Fire the enamel and allow the component to cool completely.

ADD THE SALT DESIGN

Work on a cool trivet to complete the component. Prepare a watery solution of your enamel paint color and apply it to the surface of the component **[3, 4]**. Add more water if it appears too dry.

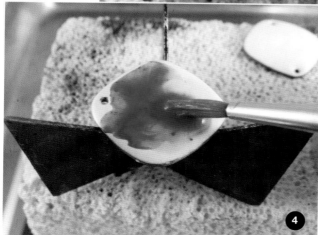

Next, carefully drop a small amount of salt onto the surface of the metal and allow the salt to absorb the paint **[5, 6]**. Let the salt/enamel paint mixture dry for about five minutes and then begin to fire **[7]**. Don't be alarmed by some of the small bits of salt jumping off of the project.

Continue to fire the component until the enamel paints are fully fused and the salt has started to settle into the background color **[8]**. Allow the component to cool before removing from the trivet **[9]**. You may notice some salt embedded into the glass, but don't worry. Once the component is completely cool, simply submerse it in water and allow the salt to dissolve **[10]**. Dry it completely.

FINISH THE BRACELET

Cut a 2-in. (5cm) piece of wire and make a plain loop on one end. String a round bead and make another plain loop. Repeat to make four bead links (or as many as needed for your bracelet). Connect the loops and components in the desired pattern. Attach a jump ring to one end of the bracelet and attach a jump ring and clasp to the other end.

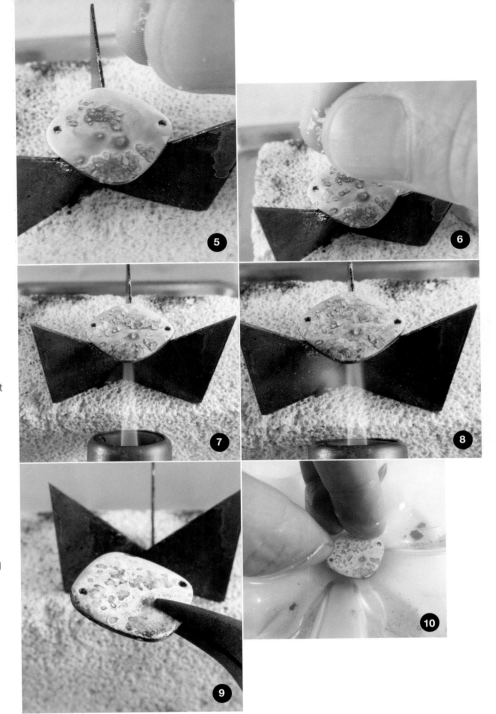

 TRY SOMETHING DIFFERENT

Once you understand the steps and are comfortable with this technique, try creating faux coral using a bright red enamel background with black paint. How about faux turquoise using a light/greenish blue with green paint?

RIVER ROCK
BRACELET

I've always been fascinated by river rocks—
there is something elegant and pure about their
look. That said, I don't know how many people
want to wear heavy rocks around their wrists.
Enter this faux-rock design, which is a much
lighter way to accessorize! Intentionally omitting
the hole gives the rocks an even more
authentic look.

YOU'LL NEED

- 1–3 18-gauge oval copper shapes in various sizes
- 24 in. (61cm) 28-gauge steel wire per rock
- Finished leather bracelet
- Counterenamel (Black)
- Enamels in shades of blue and gray (I used
  Dove Gray, Pussywillow Gray, Stump Gray, and
  Steel Gray.)
- Klyr-Fire
- Small paintbrush and rubber gloves

- Etching cream
- Small plastic bottle with lid
- Penny Brite, old toothbrush, and small towel
- Kiln brick, trivet, torch, bentnose pliers, and
  fine-point tweezers
- Sifter, dust mask, and magazine sheets
- Dapping block and hammer
- Hole-punching pliers
- Wire cutters

SHAPE THE METAL

First, using the largest dome on the dapping block, shape the oval metal piece **[1]**. Next, use a standard hammer to slightly reshape the metal. Lightly dap the sides to create a more realistic-looking shape. You can use the next dome size down to further shape the metal.

COUNTERENAMEL

Once the metal has been shaped to your liking, prepare the backside (concave side) as in "Cleaning Your Copper," p. 16 **[2]**. Counterenamel it **[3, 4]**. Allow it to cool and then remove the firescale from the front side (convex side) of the metal.

ENAMEL

As there are no holes on the metal, it might be helpful to use a small bottle to support the piece as you apply the enamel to the domed piece. You may also simply balance the metal on your index finger. Begin by applying a thin layer of Klyr-Fire **[5]** and then sift on the selected enamel color **[6]**. Carefully place the metal on the trivet and fire **[7]**. If the metal isn't fully

NOTE

A metal dapping block can be quite an investment. I prefer to splurge on my enamels, so I use a very basic and affordable block. It works perfectly fine.

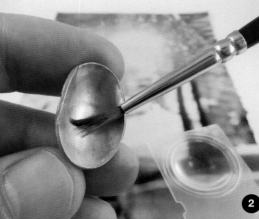

covered with enamel, allow it to cool and repeat the sifting process. Once the metal is fully covered, allow it to cool, and then place it on a paper towel.

ETCH

Etching is the secret for giving enamel a matte look to resemble river rocks. Etching cream is very caustic, so do not work with it without wearing a pair of rubber gloves. Place the component on a lid or other protective surface. Using a paintbrush and a pair of fine-point tweezers, apply a layer of etching cream over the component **[8]**. Immediately rinse the tweezers under running water to remove the etchant. Allow the component to sit five to seven minutes. Then (while still wearing the gloves) rinse the metal, removing all of the etching cream from the surface. Dry.

FINISH THE BRACELET

To complete this project, use 28-gauge steel to wire wrap the component around a simple leather band. First, punch a hole in the middle of the bracelet (or, if you are using multiple components, punch holes where desired), and add a small, tight overhand knot to the end of the wire. Bring the wire through the front of the leather and then back over the component for several wraps. Finish by trimming and tucking the end of the wire under the wraps on the back side of the cuff.

 TRY SOMETHING DIFFERENT

The matte finish is key to creating the look of stone, but you can also add matte texture to the surface of your faux stone by under-firing a top coat of enamel. Complete all of the sifting steps above. Once you have an even layer of fused enamel on the metal, add an additional thin layer of enamel and fire it until it is just past the sugar-coat stage (see "Sugar Coat It Necklace," p. 38, for more instruction). Allow the project to cool and then complete the etching process.

Ready to Raku
Bracelet

My parents lived in Japan for several years. It was during that time I fell in love with the look of raku. People often think it is only a ceramic technique, and while raku is part of the ceramic family, it is quite possible to get raku-like looks with enamels. It requires a special recipe, as well as some of my favorite twists on the technique—such as using dried rosemary. Use this recipe and special technique to add a raku finish to any piece of copper.

YOU'LL NEED

- 4 copper plumbing tubes, ¾ in. (1.9cm) long
- 24 8mm jump rings
- 2-strand tube bar clasp
- Black opaque counterenamel
- Base opaque enamel color (I used Ivory and Sky Blue.)
- "Raku recipe" transparent enamels: Turquoise, Beryl Green, Nile Green, and Peacock Green
- Klyr-Fire
- French shears

- Firing pot (You'll need a small, unlined can, ceramic tiles, small sheets of newspaper, and a generous teaspoon of completely dried rosemary.)
- Water bowl, Penny Brite, old toothbrush, and small towel
- Kiln brick, trivet, torch, bentnose pliers, and fine-point tweezers
- Sifter, dust mask, and magazine sheets
- 2 pairs of chainnose pliers
- Hole-punching pliers

PREPARE THE METAL

Anneal the tubes **[1]**. Once they cool, use French shears to cut the tubes into thirds **[2]**. As you cut the components, they might curl—so use a pair of bentnose pliers to reshape them as needed. Make 10–12 components (my bracelet has 11). Repeat the following steps for each component. First, use hole-punching pliers to make four holes in the component—one in each corner **[3]**.

COUNTERENAMEL

Prepare the backside of the component as in "Cleaning Your Copper," p. 16. Let it dry before adding the counterenamel. Apply a thin coat of Klyr-Fire to the backside of the component **[4]** and sift on the counterenamel **[5]**. Carefully place on the trivet and fire the counterenamel. Repeat this step until the backside is covered with enamel. Set the component aside to cool. (As you work, you can set the cooled pieces into a citric-acid bath to help remove the firescale.) Clean the front side of the component, thoroughly.

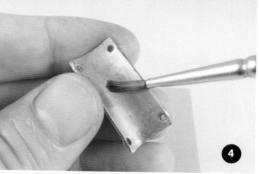

PREPARE TO ENAMEL

The raku finish, especially the copper finish, is a result of a specific combination of enamels, with much of the heavy lifting coming from the turquoise color **[6]**. It is a transparent enamel—in fact, all of the enamels in the "raku recipe" are transparent. I prefer to sift light-colored opaque enamel **[7]** onto the metal first (I used Ivory for this sample), followed by a random placement of the transparent colors. The key to remember for this technique is the turquoise color is the ticket. You'll get far more metallic shine when using more turquoise, but the other colors kick in to produce different results. Always be open to the fact that the outcome is rather difficult to control.

Before you begin enameling, you need to create a fire pot. If you've seen traditional raku in action, it can be quite intimidating, but I use a common aluminum can and a ceramic tile for my fire pot. First, use shears to cut the can in half. Try to cut an even line around the can, so the tile will fit snugly when placed on top. Fill your fire pot with small strips of newspaper, about 1-in. (2.5cm) long and ½ in. (1.3cm) wide. I also add a few dried rosemary leaves **[8]**. it creates a far more pleasant smell, and sometimes the rosemary gets stuck to the enamel, creating an amazing texture on the piece. This project does create smoke, so work either in a well-ventilated area or outside, and watch for smoke detectors.

FIRE

Fire the piece all the way to fully fused **[9, 10, 11]**. Continue to fire, then drop the piece into the fire pot, trivet and all **[12]**. Use a pair of bentnose pliers to transfer the copper component to the firing pot. Try and maintain a high level of heat on the project. Use your non-dominant hand to hold the torch and your dominant hand to transfer the metal to the firing pot. If the metal "sticks" to the trivel, simply add both the trivet and metal to the firepot. Once cooled, you can separate the trivet and component.

Ideally, the metal will cause the paper (combustible material) to ignite—if not, point the torch towards the newspaper to do so. Once the paper is on fire, extinguish the flame by placing the ceramic tile over the top of the fire pot **[13]**. Allow it to sit a for a few minutes, and then carefully remove the tile (it will be hot). I often grab the tile from the edges. Set the tile aside and use fine-point tweezers to remove the metal from the pot. Allow the metal to cool, and don't worry if the outcome is too dark— sometimes the metallic shine can be covered by soot, which is easily re- moved with a gentle rub. Raku work is best left all on its own; avoid the temptation to clean the project.

FINISH
THE BRACELET

Connect the components with jump rings at the top and bottom. Attach a bar clasp to each end of the bracelet with jump rings.

 TRY SOMETHING DIFFERENT

The raku finish is beautiful, and the delight of pulling out projects from the fire pot is a great feeling. Consider using the raku finish on several of the projects throughout the book! I think the finish is well-suited to many of the pieces, so consider taking your new raku skills one step further.

Working With Wire

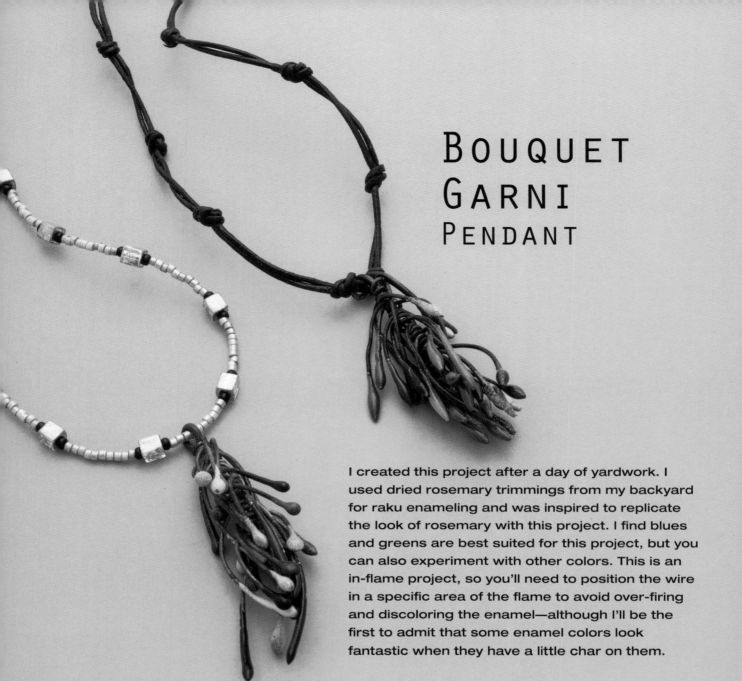

BOUQUET GARNI PENDANT

I created this project after a day of yardwork. I used dried rosemary trimmings from my backyard for raku enameling and was inspired to replicate the look of rosemary with this project. I find blues and greens are best suited for this project, but you can also experiment with other colors. This is an in-flame project, so you'll need to position the wire in a specific area of the flame to avoid over-firing and discoloring the enamel—although I'll be the first to admit that some enamel colors look fantastic when they have a little char on them.

YOU'LL NEED

- 20 2–3-in. (5–7.6mm) pieces of 20-gauge copper wire
- 3 in. (7.6cm) 18-gauge copper wire
- Beading wire or leather cord necklace
- Opaque enamels (choose colors within the same family for maximum effect)
- Kiln brick, trivet, torch, bentnose pliers, and cross-locking tweezers
- Sifter, dust mask, and magazine sheets
- Shallow glass bowl or saucer to hold loose enamel (1 for each color)
- Roundnose pliers and chainnose pliers
- Wire cutters
- Vermiculite in a container

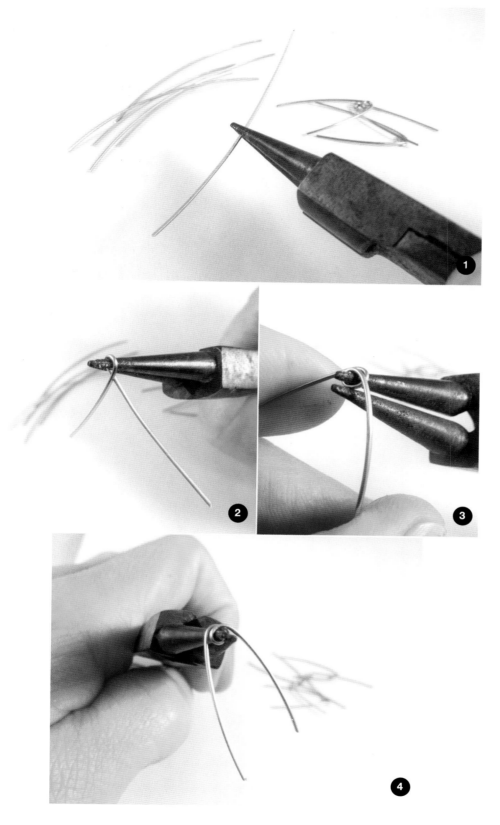

PREPARE THE WIRE

Before beginning your project, you'll need to create one 3-in. stem as well as about twenty 2–3-in. branches. Leave the stem straight. To create a branch, center a pair of roundnose pliers on each wire and wrap the end of each wire one full rotation around the pliers' jaws **[1, 2, 3, 4]**. Create various lengths of the branches, as the pieces will be stacked over each other. If your wire has a tarnish-resistant coating, pass the wire through the torch flame to burn off the coating (Make sure you're in a well-ventilated space!). Now, your wires are ready to be enameled.

Enamel the Stem

Place the enamel color you want to use in a glass container. With a pair of cross-locking tweezers, prepare the stem by heating the tip (end) of the wire until it is orange in color, forming a small ball at the end. Next, turn the wire around so the balled end is facing away from the flame tip and reheat until orange in color. Immediately immerse the end in enamel **[5]** and be sure to get even coverage on the tip. If you dip too far and aren't consistent with the depth, the enamel will be too thin in certain sections and may break off the wire. Repeat **[6]** until the tip is coated with enamel, most likely 7–12 dips.

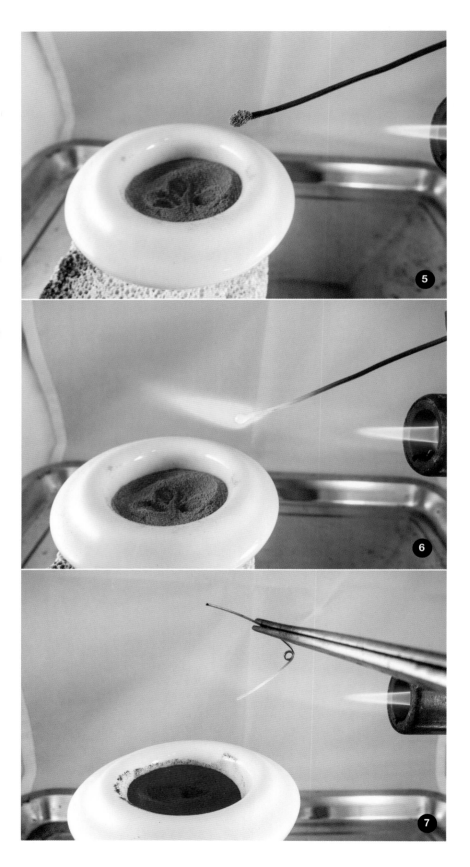

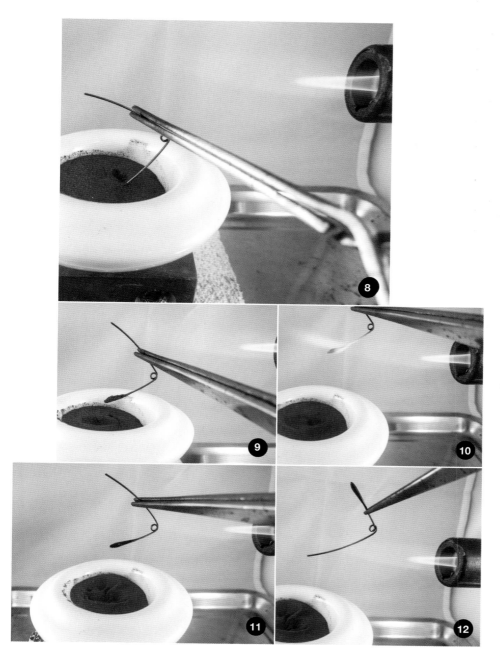

ENAMEL THE BRANCHES

Set the wire in the vermiculite and begin working with the branches. Heat one tip of a branch **[7]**. The end of the wire should be facing away from the flame tip. To avoid heating the opposite end of the stem, bend it up, out of the direction of the flame. Add enamel to the branch the same way you added enamel to the stem **[8, 9, 10, 11]**. Add enamel to both wire ends on each branch **[12]**. When finished, place each branch in the vermiculite and allow it to cool.

FINISH THE PENDANT

Thread all 20 branches onto the stem. You might need to reposition them for even coverage. The wire is very malleable, so form the piece so the branches rest on each other. As you add more and more branches, the pendant will begin to fill out. Once all branches are in place, make a plain loop at the top of the stem, ensuring the end of the loop helps lock in the branches so they don't move vertically along the stem. String the pendant on a simple leather cord or on beading wire as desired.

 TRY SOMETHING DIFFERENT

Consider making two smaller versions of the project to use as a pair of earrings. You can also cluster more than one pendant on a necklace.

CONNECT THE DOTS
EARRINGS

After you've made a few projects with wire, you can actually create what I refer to as an organic and colorful chain-link earring. Each link has an end covered in glass, helping connect the components and hold them in place.

YOU'LL NEED

- 18–20 2-in. 22-gauge copper headpins
- Pair of earring wires
- Opaque enamel in various colors (red, orange, yellow, blue, and green)
- Small glass container, one for each color used in the project
- Penny Brite, old toothbrush and small toweo
- Kiln brick, trivet, torch, bentnose pliers, and fine-point tweezers
- Sifter, dust mask, and magazine sheets
- Vermiculite bowl
- Roundnose pliers, chainnose pliers, and bentnose pliers
- Wire cutters

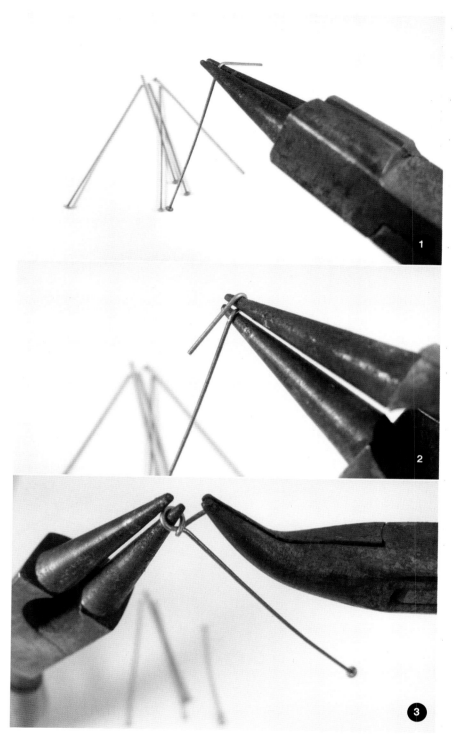

PREPARE THE WIRE

When working with copper headpins, keep in mind they might have an anti-tarnish coating on them. You'll want to burn it off before you work with the wire. A quick pass through your torch flame will remove this coating. (Be sure you're working in an area with good ventilation.)

WRAP THE WIRE

After the pieces have cooled, create a wrapped loop at the end of each headpin **[1, 2, 3]**. This project is less about wire wrapping and more about enameling, so less-than-professional wraps are acceptable here—you simply need a closed loop. In fact, the funkier the wrap, the more successful the result.

ENAMEL

Have your enamel ready in glass containers, as you'll be dipping into the enamel for this project. The firing process is similar to the technique used in the "Bouquet Garni Pendant," p. 56; however, this time you're working with connected pieces of wire. Feed the wrapped headpin through the loop of another headpin. Use fine-point tweezers to hold the second headpin away from the end of the first headpin **[4]**.

Now, carefully hold the end of the headpin so it is directly in the flame to heat up the copper and form a small balled end **[5]**. Once you have a balled-up end, you are ready to add enamel to it. Heat the balled-up end until it is orange in color and then immediately immerse into the enamel **[6]**. Bring it back up to the flame and fire it until the enamel fully flows and is orange in color. Continue this process until the end of the first headpin is unable to slide through the loop of the second wire **[7]**. (Remember, if the enamel is too thin, it may chip off.)

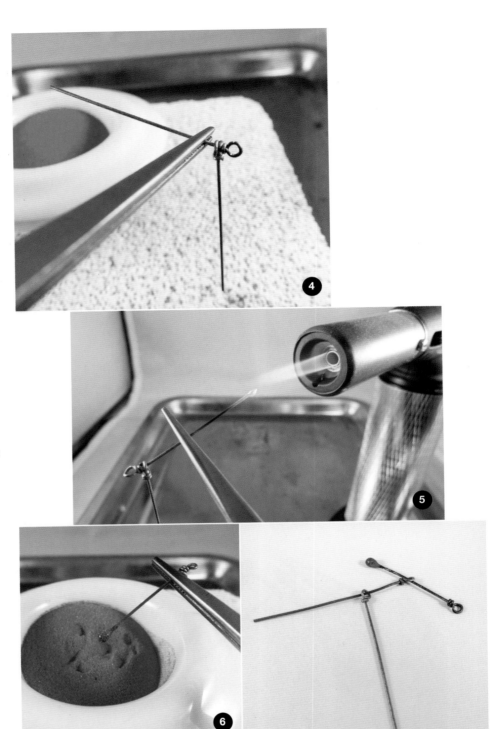

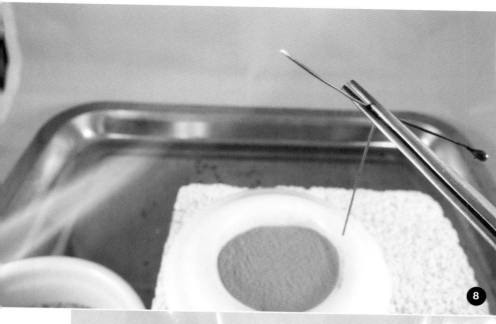

Place the headpins in the vermiculite. Begin to assemble the earring chain by repeating the enameling process, connecting headpins together to make a chain **[8]**. I connected my headpins together so they created three "branches" made of three or four headpins each.

Carefully clean the connected headpins in a Penny Brite bath to remove any excess firescale **[9]**.

FINISH THE EARRINGS

For each earring, attach an earring wire to the loops at the top of the chains. (I used three per earring.)

 TRY SOMETHING DIFFERENT

You can take the simplicity of this design even further! If you're up to the challenge, consider making a 1-yd. rope-length version. Wrapping the chain around your neck will be visually stunning and show the world you're a master at creating enameled chain!

COCOON EARRINGS

When you encase fine-silver wire within transparent enamel, you'll create a collection of wonderfully colored components. Cool colors, such as transparent blue and green enamels, are best for this project, as warm colors like red and yellow interact with the fine silver to create less dynamic results (the colors get muddied).

YOU'LL NEED

- 1 yd. (.9m) 20-gauge fine-silver wire (enough to make 16 components for each earring)
- 2 2-in. (5cm) sterling silver headpins
- Pair of earring wires
- Transparent enamel (You can use the same greens from the "Ready to Raku Bracelet," p. 50.)
- Penny Brite, old toothbrush, and small towel

- Kiln brick, trivet, torch, bentnose pliers, and cross-locking tweezers
- Sifter, dust mask, and magazine sheets
- Vermiculite in a container
- Roundnose pliers and chainnose or bentnose pliers
- Wire cutters

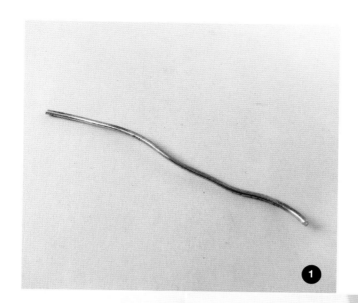

PREPARE the WIRE

You will create all of the cocoons before adding the enamels. First, cut the wire into 1½-in. (3.8cm) pieces, making sure both ends are flush cut **[1]**. To create the wrap sections of the cocoon, begin to bend the wire onto itself. Use bentnose pliers to begin a loop **[2]**, then wrap it over itself. Continue to do so **[3, 4]** until there is a ½-in. (1.3cm) section of wire left **[5]**.

FIRE the WIRE

Use cross-locking tweezers to hold the wire in front of the flame, at the far end of the tip of the flame. With your non-dominant hand, hold the wire in the flame, while using your dominant hand to hold the sifting cup.

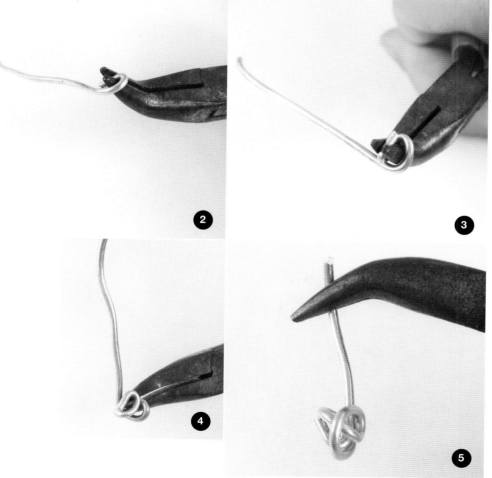

As the wire heats up to a dull orange color, quickly pull the wire out of the flame and add the enamel to the surface of the wire **[6]**. Continue to fire until the enamel has set **[7]**. Repeat this process until the coiled section of the cocoon is completely covered with enamel. Once the cocoon is covered in color, place the cocoon inside the vermiculite and allow it to cool completely.

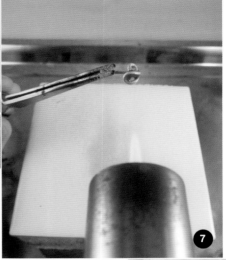

FINISH THE EARRINGS

Make a plain loop on the end of each cocoon component **[8]**. String 16 cocoons on a silver headpin **[9]**. Avoid layering the components in the same direction, flipping them over so they lay correctly. Make a wrapped loop at the top of the headpin. Connect an earring wire. Repeat to make a second earring.

NOTE
You can use the same transparent enamel from the raku recipe: Turquoise, Beryl Green, Nile Green, and Peacock Green. You might also consider Gem Green and Grass Green, too!

 TRY SOMETHING DIFFERENT

Silver prices are always fluctuating, which is one of the reasons I rarely use it for enameling. But when the price is right, I like to stock up. If you have the budget and the inclination, consider creating a set of cocoons to string on a necklace—this design will emerge as a clear winner!

DNA Pendant

Once you've mastered working with wire, you can work with a smaller gauge of wire to create this pendant. It reminds me of a DNA strand, but you may see something different. I discovered the color "Sapphire" a few years back, and it is now one of my favorites. Students adore this color because it is an incredible complement to the natural color of copper. As you create this project, you should use the colors you enjoy best—but Sapphire is certainly one to add to your collection!

YOU'LL NEED

- Approximately 8 ft. (2.4m) 26-gauge copper wire
- 12 in. (30cm) 20-gauge wire
- 18 in. (46cm) 1.5mm leather cording
- 2 6mm jump rings
- 2 crimp ends
- Lobster claw clasp
- Opaque enamel (I used Sapphire.)

- Penny Brite, old toothbrush, and small towel
- Kiln brick, trivet, torch, bentnose pliers, and cross-locking tweezers
- Sifter, dust mask, and magazine sheets
- Vermiculite in a container
- Roundnose pliers and chainnose pliers
- Wire cutters

PREPARE THE WIRE

When working with wire, remember it may be coated with anti-tarnish protection. Be sure to burn it off before you work with the wire. A quick pass through your torch flame will remove the coating (be sure to work in a well-ventilated room). Once the 26-gauge wire has cooled, cut it into 1-in. (2.5cm) pieces. (The number of wire pieces you'll need may vary, but you'll need at least 100.) Cut the 20-gauge wire into five pieces: one 3-in. (7.6cm) two 2½-in. (6.4cm), and two 1½-in. (3.8cm) long.

ENAMEL THE 20-GAUGE WIRE

This firing process is similar to the technique used in the "Bouquet Garni Pendant," p. 56. Ball up one end of each 20-gauge piece of wire **[1]**. Add enamel to the balled-up end as in the "Bouquet Garni Pendant." Once covered with enamel, place the wire in the vermiculite and let cool.

ENAMEL THE 26-GAUGE WIRE

Place the enamel in a glass container. Choose a wire and bend it into a U shape, with both sides the same length **[2]**. This allows you to create balled-up ends at the same time and also immerse both ends into the enamel, simultaneously.

Use cross-locking tweezers to hold the wire at its midpoint **[3]**. Begin to ball one end **[4]**. Be sure to monitor the wire—as it is a thinner gauge, with a risk of melting more than usual. Ball up one end, and then turn the wire around to ball up the other end. Once both ends are done, set the wire on the kiln brick to cool.

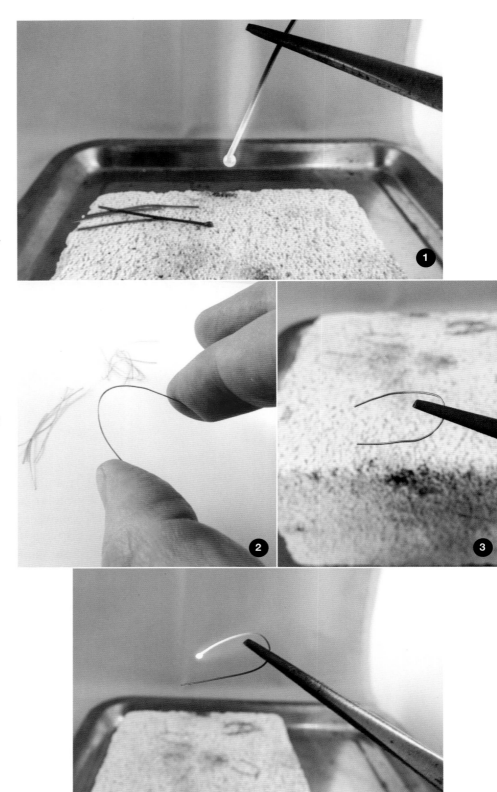

Now, use the tweezers to hold the end of the wire in the far end of the flame. Once the wire tips glow orange **[5]**, immediately immerse them into the enamel **[6]**. Continue the process about five times **[7]** or until you have covered the ends well with enamel. (If the coating is too thin, the enamel may chip off.) Once covered with enamel, place the wire in the vermiculite and let it cool **[8]**.

If you're anxious to enamel the wire, work in batches. Create about 10 pieces of wire and then enamel them before making more.

FINISH THE NECKLACE

To create the DNA strands, curl the 26-gauge wire components around the 20-gauge core wire. Wrap tightly and continue until you have ¼ in. (6mm) left **[9]**. Make a plain loop on the core wire. Repeat to make five DNA strands. String the strands on the leather cord. (I randomly added a few extra components on the main leather cord as well.) Crimp a crimp clasp to each end. Attach a lobster claw clasp to one end with a jump ring. Add a jump ring at the other end.

 TRY SOMETHING DIFFERENT

Creating the longer center core wires first, gives you an idea of what you'll need to do if you decide to make more core wires. I think a necklace looks just as fantastic with one core wire, as it does with three or five. Don't hesitate to change the design—you can keep it simple, yet sophisticated.

NOTE
Use crimp ends to connect the leather cord to the clasp.

Enameled-Wire Word Pendants

I love this project because of its simplicity. There is also a high level of personal expression when a single word is dangled from a colored cord. Black enamel 1995 is the BEST enamel for this project. I've tried other colors with mixed results, but I encourage you to prove me wrong!

You'll need

- 12 in. (30cm) 20-gauge copper wire (for each word)
- 8mm jump ring (for each word)
- Pre-finished, suede cord necklace
- Black enamel in a flat saucer on flat glass plate (I used 1955.)
- Penny Brite, old toothbrush, and small towel

- Roundnose pliers, bentnose pliers, and chainnose pliers
- Kiln brick, trivet, torch, and cross-locking tweezers
- Sifter, dust mask
- Wire cutters
- Vermiculite in a container

PREPARE THE WIRE

This project is all about self-expression, so consider which words you want to use. Keep in mind the words you create should never be longer than 2 in. (5cm). I like to anneal the wire first, so it is easier to manipulate **[1]**.

It is also helpful to draw the word on paper first, so you're familiar with the direction you'll need to bend the wire **[2]**. Write in cursive, create tight connections between the letters, and NEVER use more than one piece of wire **[3, 4]**. As you create the word, make sure to leave a small "tail" you can hold during the enameling process. This tail should stretch out from the beginning or ending of the word.

NOTE

You might want to practice the word-creation process with craft wire. If you have a wire go *haywire*, you can use a wire straightener to start all over again.

Enamel

This process requires you to immerse the wire into the black enamel, so have your enamel ready to go in a flat saucer on a flat glass plate. Set the torch to the side of the immersion plate and lower the wire into the far end of the flame. Once the wire is glowing orange, immediately dip it into the enamel **[5]**. Gently tap off the excess enamel and then bring the wire back into the flame **[6]**. Fire until the enamel has fully fused, then immediately immerse the wire into the enamel again **[7]**. Make sure you have an even layer of enamel on the piece. You might need to adjust how you immerse the wire, based on the coverage **[8]**. You might also need to carefully sift enamel onto the wire; be mindful of the flame to avoid burning the sifting cup **[9]**. Once the wire is sufficiently covered, place the wire in the vermiculite and allow it to cool.

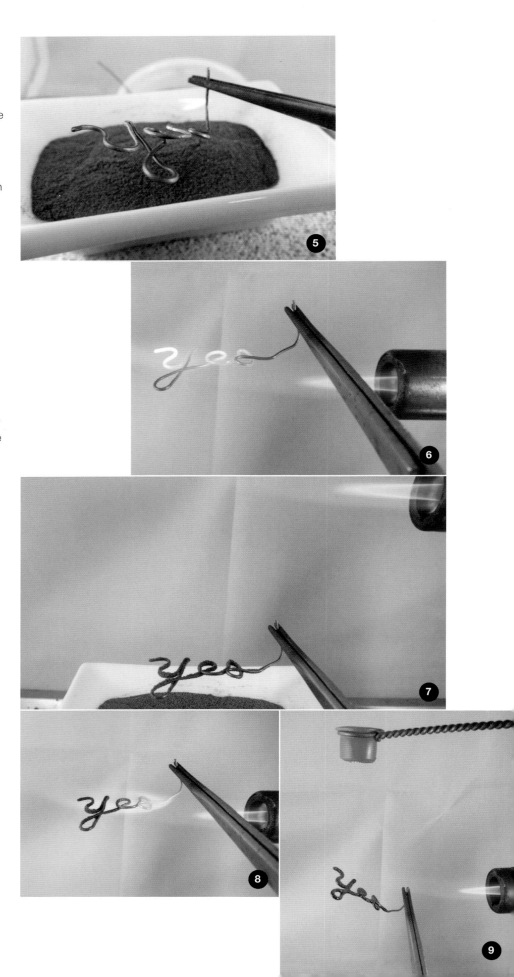

FINISH THE COMPONENT

To remove the wire tail, use flush wire cutters to cut it off with one swift, clean cut [10]. You'll now fix the end of the wire, covering it with more black enamel. Holding the project on the farthest point from the cut end, place the exposed tip in the flame. Heat just THIS area [11] and dip THIS area only into the black enamel [12]. Continue to do so until the area is covered, then return to the vermiculite. Allow to cool.

FINISH THE PIECE

Open a jump ring and slide it through a loop near the top of your component. Attach the jump ring to the suede cord for a lovely pendant.

 ## TRY SOMETHING DIFFERENT

This is one of my favorite projects. I encourage designers to treat these components as wearable works of art. I think the design works well on its own, but I also think one could layer several necklaces to create a really dramatic statement.

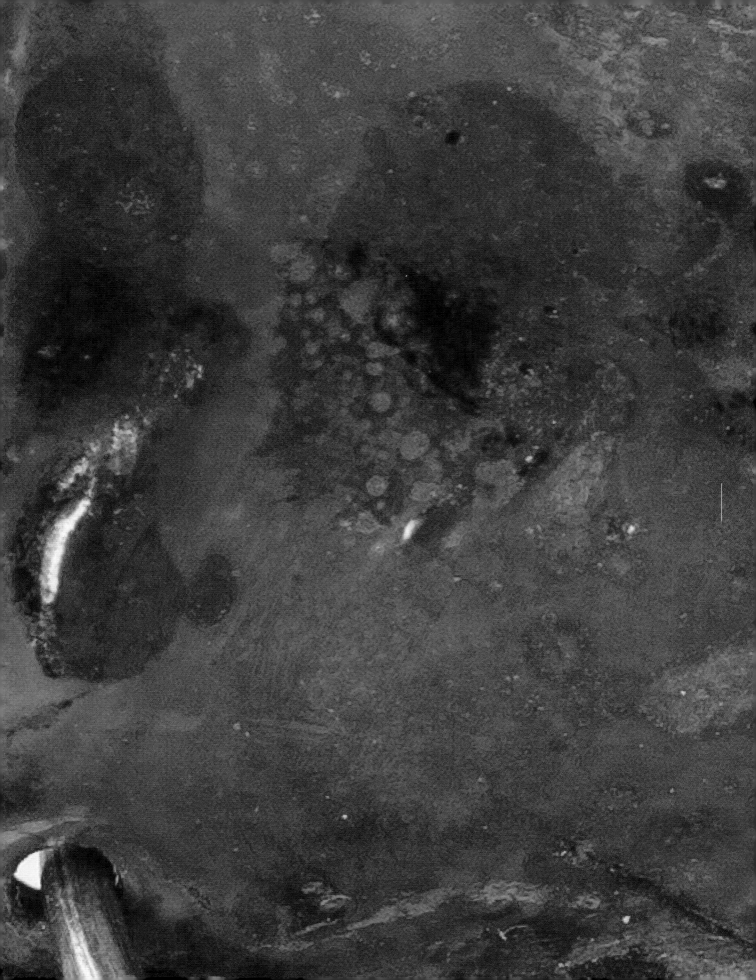

MANIPULATING
METAL

DIMENSIONAL DESIGNS
PENDANT

This has always been a popular class—students love how it combines sculptural elements with very basic soldering. As with many of my projects, it allows for quick and easy customization when it comes to color selection, enameling techniques, and the shapes used in the design. There is lots of room to spread your creative wings here.

YOU'LL NEED

- Copper disks: 35mm, 16mm, and 10mm
- 30 4mm beads
- 18 in. (46cm) 20-gauge wire
- 22 5mm jump rings
- Toggle clasp
- Opaque enamel and counterenamel (I used Marigold and Orient Red.)
- Water bowl, Penny Brite, old toothbrush, and small towel

- Solder-It copper bearing paste
- Kiln brick, trivet, torch, fine-point tweezers, and titanium pick
- Klyr-Fire
- Sifter, dust mask, and magazine sheets
- Hole-punching pliers and wire cutters
- Dapping block
- Scalex with small paintbrush
- Roundnose pliers, bentnose pliers, and chainnose pliers

PREPARE THE METAL

The largest disk will remain flat, while the two smaller disks will be domed. First, punch a hole near the top edge of the largest disk for the jump ring to fit through.

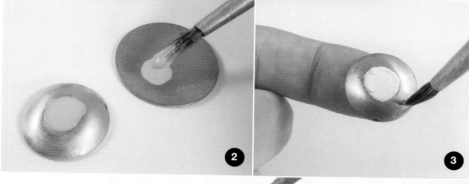

Next, form the smaller metal disks in the dapping block **[1]**. Place them dome-side up, one at a time on the steel bench block, and lightly tap the backside of each piece so there is a small, flattened area. Place the smaller disks on the larger piece to determine their location on the finished project. Clean the backside of both domed disks. Apply Scalex on the front of the largest disk and the back of the smaller disks where the pieces will meet **[2]**. This product prevents firescale and will create an enamel-free area for the solder. Let the Scalex dry.

COUNTERENAMEL

Clean the backside of the largest disk, add counterenamel, and allow to cool. Then place the disk in a citric acid bath to help remove the firescale.

Add Klyr-Fire to the back of the small domed disks **[3]**. Sift on a layer of counterenamel, and then use a dry paintbrush to gently remove the enamel from the area covered with Scalex **[4]**. (If the smaller disks are less than a quarter-inch in diameter, you can skip the counterenamel. Pieces larger than this should be counterenameled.) Fire the disks **[5]** and allow them to cool.

ENAMEL THE LARGEST DISK

Clean the front side of the largest (flat) disk. Allow it to dry, and then add Scalex to the areas you'll use to connect the smaller disks. Allow it to dry, and then sift the enamel onto the piece, doing your best to cover the Scalex completely **[6]**. Carefully place it on the trivet and then fire it **[7]**. Allow to cool. Create the "sgraffito" look by sifting a second color on top of the first and using a pick to draw lines through the top color **[8]**. (The Scalex might pop off after the first fire. If this happens, reapply the Scalex or during the second sift; avoid covering the bare copper spots with enamel.) Remove the enamel from the Scalex **[9]**, and then fire it **[10]**. Let the largest disk cool.

ENAMEL THE SMALLER DISKS

Once the small disks are cool, place them in a citric acid bath until they're clean. Remove them and dry them off. Apply a thin coat of Klyr-Fire to the concave side of one piece **[11]** and then sift on the enamel **[12]**. To avoid leaving a mark in the counterenamel, turn the trivet over and place the metal in the center

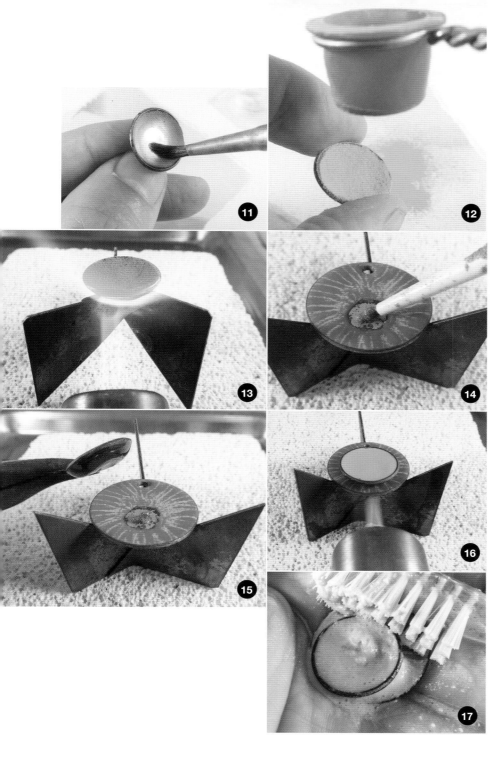

of the trivet. Fire until the enamel fully flows **[13]**. Let it cool, and then remove the piece from the trivet. When all metal pieces are enameled, remove the firescale from the bare areas of the piece with Penny Brite, as you'll need a clean connection between the metals before soldering.

SOLDER

Apply a small amount of the solder paste to the larger piece **[14]** and place the smaller pieces on top **[15]**. You'll want to fire all solder connections at the same time. Keep in mind the solder has a lower melting point than the enamel, so you don't need the same level of flame you would use for enamel. Gently heat the project, allowing the solder to flow **[16]**. The project should cool for several minutes before you remove it from the trivet. Don't be alarmed by the flux residue, which appears when you fire this particular brand of solder. Gently clean the piece with Penny Brite, as well as with warm sudsy water to remove all of the flux residue **[17]**.

FINISH THE NECKLACE

Make bead links by stringing one or two beads on the 20-gauge wire and making a plain loop on each end. Connect the links with jump rings. Use a jump ring to connect the pendant to a jump ring in the center of the necklace. Connect half of a toggle clasp to each end of the necklace with a jump ring.

 TRY SOMETHING DIFFERENT

There are so many ways to approach this project. The many different copper shapes available allow a designer to create several types of jewelry. If you are new to soldering, I encourage you to only add one piece of metal to your design as I did in the instructions, until you feel comfortable with the process. It will be stunning either way.

BUBBLE
EARRINGS

Once you start working with copper pipe, you'll be surprised how easy it is to use in a variety of projects. Here, you'll use copper refrigerator coil to create a colorful pair of bubble earrings. Colors are such a personal choice for people, but I find monochromatic colors provide the most stunning effect with this design. This project is a take on plique-a-jour (French for "letting in light"), but instead of using transparent enamels, I'm using opaque colors.

YOU'LL NEED

- ¼-in. (6mm) diameter refrigerator copper tubing
- 2 pieces of ½-in. (1.3cm) copper tubes
- 2 2-in. (5cm) headpins
- Pair of earring wires
- Opaque enamels and counterenamel
- Tube cutter and diamond file
- Line sifter (optional)
- Small sheets of mica, 1x1 in. (2.5x2.5cm)

- Water bowl, Penny Brite, old toothbrush, titanium pick, and small towel
- Kiln brick, trivet, torch, and fine-point tweezers
- Stay-Brite coil solder and hammer
- Sifter, dust mask, and magazine sheets
- Hole-punching pliers
- Chainnose pliers, roundnose pliers, and bentnose pliers
- Wire cutters

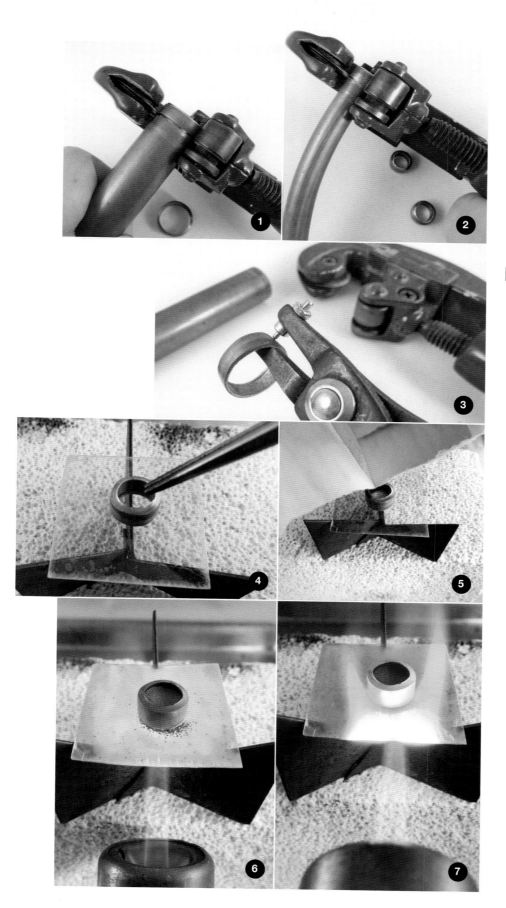

Prepare the Copper

Use the tube cutter to create two ½-in. (1.3cm) pipe cut-outs **[1]**. You'll also need six ¼-in. (6mm) cut-outs **[2]**. Each should be approximately ⅛ in. (3mm) high. Punch a hole in the center of the largest ring **[3]**. Soak the pieces in a citric acid bath. Allow them to dry before adding the enamel.

Enamel

Place a mica square on a stainless steel trivet. Place a single piece of tube on top of the mica square **[4]**. Carefully add enamel to the inside of the tube (fill it about halfway) using a line sifter or a folded piece of magazine paper **[5]**. Avoid disturbing the placement of the tube to ensure the enamel will stay inside the tube. Don't worry about enamel falling onto the front of the tube, as you can remove this with a diamond file after you've finished firing.

You're now ready for the first firing. Mica is able to withstand a tremendous amount of heat, but the flame's first contact with the sheet will slightly warp and discolor the mica. Slowly introduce the flame into the project area, directing it under the tube **[6]**. After about a minute, redirect the flame to the side of the tube, keeping in mind the flame should not enter the inside of the tube **[7]**. Pay close attention to the enamel, as it will slowly fuse to the sides, and in most cases, settle to the bottom of the tube. Allow the tube to cool. Add a second layer of enamel inside the tube **[8]**.

Do not overfill the tube or you'll likely burn the exposed enamel.

Tap down the unfired enamel with a titanium pick **[9]**. Fire the tube once again. Allow it to cool and carefully remove the tube from the mica. You should be able to use the mica for a few more fires, but use a new piece if it disintegrates or becomes too unstable to use. Add enamel to all the small tubes.

FILE

Once all of the pieces are fired, smooth the backsides of each component with a diamond file **[10]**. This not only removes the loose mica, but also levels the enamels. Once filed, prepare to solder by cleaning all connection points and filing away any firescale **[11]**. Arrange your design upside down, as you'll solder from the backside of the piece. Apply Stay-Brite to the planned connection points **[12]**.

Working in sections, slowly solder the tubes together by adding small chips of the solder wire to the connection points **[13]**. You can turn solder wire into chips by hammering them flat. Use tweezers to position them and use a lower flame to melt the solder into place. Allow to cool for several minutes before removing the project from the brick.

When complete, use Penny Brite to thoroughly clean the project and remove flux residue.

FINISH THE EARRINGS

For each earring, insert a headpin through the bottom of the largest ring and attach to an earring wire with a wrapped loop.

 TRY SOMETHING DIFFERENT

The design of this project is incredibly versatile. Before you solder the pieces together, try bold patterns or keep it simple and make a pair of earrings with just a few pieces. A smaller project is a great way to practice the technique. You might also consider some of the pattern ideas for pendant projects, too! The key is ensuring the solder connection points are clean and touching each other.

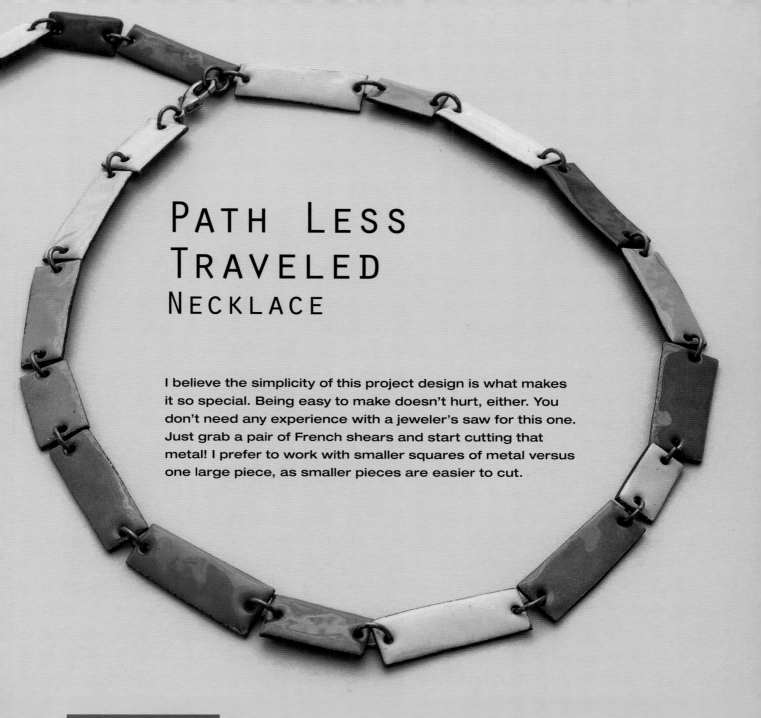

PATH LESS TRAVELED
NECKLACE

I believe the simplicity of this project design is what makes it so special. Being easy to make doesn't hurt, either. You don't need any experience with a jeweler's saw for this one. Just grab a pair of French shears and start cutting that metal! I prefer to work with smaller squares of metal versus one large piece, as smaller pieces are easier to cut.

YOU'LL NEED

- 4 or 5 1-in. (2.5cm) copper squares
- Various opaque enamels (I used Cobalt Blue, Sky Blue, French Blue, Steel Grey, Darkest Blue, and Ozone Blue.)
- Black counterenamel
- 20 6mm jump rings and lobster claw clasp
- French shears
- Penny Brite, old toothbrush, and small towel

- Kiln brick, trivet, torch, and fine-point tweezers
- Sifter, dust mask, and magazine sheets
- Hole-punching pliers and bentnose pliers
- Permanent marker, straight edge, and toothpicks
- 2 pairs of chainnose pliers
- Metal file

PREPARE THE METAL

Anneal the copper squares so they are easier to cut with the shears. Place them on the kiln brick and bring them to a bright red glow. Allow them to cool and then quench them in a bowl of water. Dry off and use a marker and straight edge to create rectangular shapes about 1x¼ in. (25x6mm). Next, use the shears to cut the rectangles **[1, 2]**. They will curl as you cut them, but that's OK— simply use a hammer and a bench block to flatten them out **[3]**.

Add a 1.25mm hole to each end of the individual pieces. As you're working with smaller pieces, it might be helpful to practice placing them on the trivet. If not placed securely, they have a tendency to fall off during the firing process. Spend some time figuring out the best placement for the rectangles on the trivet.

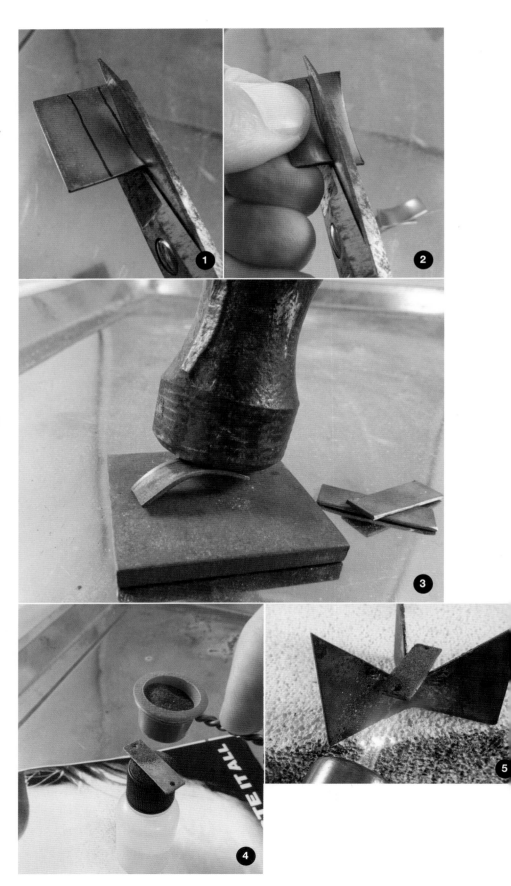

COUNTERENAMEL

Clean the backside of the each rectangle. Apply the counterenamel **[4]**. These are smaller pieces, so be sure to clear out the holes with something as simple as a toothpick so they are free of enamel. You might even consider using a small plastic bottle to hold the metal as you sift. This allows you to easily pick up the metal and place in on the trivet. After the first fire, the trivet will be hot, so be careful as you place the metal. Fire the counterenamel and allow the piece to cool **[5]**. Remove the metal from the trivet, allow the metal to cool completely, and then clean the front side of the metal.

ENAMEL

You're now ready to add color to the front. Repeat the same sifting process as with the counterenamel, fire **[6]**, and cool. Once all of the pieces are fired, file the edges.

FINISH THE NECKLACE

A simple jump ring connection is all you need to pull this project together. Attach the rectangles with jump rings, one by one **[7]**, until you reach the desired length. Add a lobster claw clasp to one end.

TRY SOMETHING DIFFERENT

The simplicity of these pieces is perfect. I've created earrings and simple pendants with just one rectangle. You can also group them together and suspend them from a necklace for a different, yet effective design.

Spellbound
Pendant

One of my first-published craft projects was a bulletin board made from a repurposed Scrabble game. I've seen countless jewelry projects inspired by these iconic tiles, so here's my take on one of my favorite board games. Tandy Leather manufacturers the punches you'll need to make the impression on the glass. I recommend keeping words at seven letters or less per pendant.

YOU'LL NEED

- 4 or 5 12mm rounded copper squares
- Finished beaded necklace and jump ring OR chain, 4 7mm jump rings, and lobster claw clasp
- Opaque enamel (I used Nut Brown and Black counterenamel.)
- Small plastic bottle, Penny Brite, old toothbrush, and small towel
- Basic letter stamps, ¼ in. (6mm) (I used Tandy Leather stamps.)

- Black, extra-fine tip permanent marker
- Stay-Brite coil solder
- Hole-punching pliers
- Kiln brick, trivet, torch, and fine-point tweezers
- Sifter, dust mask, and magazine sheets
- Bentnose pliers and 2 pairs of chainnose pliers
- Wire cutters

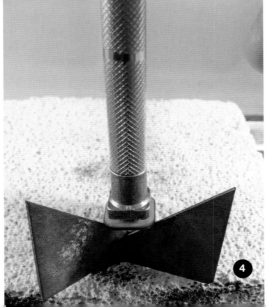

PREPARE THE COPPER

Lay out your tiles and decide how you will hang the pendant. Punch in a hole or two in the top to suspend the pendant later. For a balanced pendant: If you are working with an odd number of tiles, make a hole in the center-most tile. If you are working with an even number of tiles, create a hole on the first and last tile.

COUNTERENAMEL

Clean the backside of each square and counterenamel with black enamel. You might consider using a small plastic bottle to hold the metal as you sift—this allows you to easily pick up the metal and place in on the trivet. After the first firing, the trivet will be hot, so be careful placing the metal. Fire the counterenamel and allow the metal to cool slightly before removing it from the trivet. As these pieces are cooling, lay out your leather stamps in the order you will use them. Cool completely.

ENAMEL

Clean the front side of the metal. You're now ready to add the wood-colored enamel to the front. Repeat the same sifting process as with the counterenamel **[1]**.

Begin to fire the first tile **[2]**. You'll stamp the glass with the leather stamp once the enamel is in the final stage of fusing. This can be a bit intimidating, so practice the motion without the torch. Use your non-dominant hand to fire the tile and your dominant hand to control the leather stamp. Remember to hold the leather stamp handle at the far end—the tool is metal and it does get hot. Once the glass is bright orange, it is ready to be stamped. Remove the flame, then gently press directly into the glass, to avoid slipping or moving the stamp **[3]**. One direct press **[4]** and then quickly remove the stamp from the glass **[5]**.

Set the stamp on a protected, fire-resistant surface, and allow the tile to cool (use bentnose pliers, as the stamp will be hot) **[6]**. Remove the tile with fine-point tweezers and place it on the kiln brick to cool. Continue this process with the rest of the tiles. Once all of the pieces are fired, file the edges to remove any enamel or oxidization that might interfere with soldering.

Solder

Lay out your design on the kiln brick and then cut the solder. I use a solder called Stay-Brite coil solder, as it has a low melting point. Place a small piece of solder in the middle of each connection point **[7]**. As the solder flows, it will flow in between the tiles. Once the solder pieces are in place, add the liquid flux throughout the piece. Remember, the low melting point means you don't need a long and strong enameling flame. Fire all of the solder pieces until they flow **[8, 9]**. If you need to adjust the tiles in any way, use a titanium pick to do so, but work quickly. Allow the piece to cool completely before cleaning the it. Using a permanent marker, carefully add the paint in the impression you've created **[10]**. Allow to dry. Remove any extra paint with your fingernail.

Finish the Pendant

Use a jump ring to connect the pendant to a finished beaded necklace or attach each end to a chain and finish with a clasp.

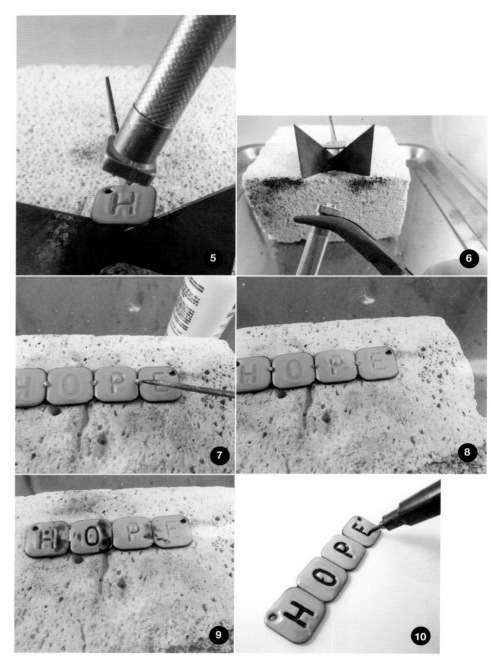

 ## Try Something Different

My projects are designed for horizontal orientation, but consider earning points with a vertically designed word. You can also cluster multiple, vertical words on a necklace.

HEARTS ON FIRE
BRACELET

Whenever I travel, I collect heart artwork. It reminds me of home. I live in San Francisco, and yes, I left my heart there long ago. This project is super easy to create and the alternating convex and concave colored shapes are very appealing.

YOU'LL NEED

- 8–10 18-gauge copper hearts, approximately 1-in. (2.5cm) wide
- 10–12 7mm jump rings
- Lobster claw clasp
- Counterenamel (I used Black.)
- Opaque enamels (I used Orient Red, Victoria Red, Flame Red, Foxglove Purple, and Clover Pink.)
- Penny Brite, old toothbrush, and small towel
- Kiln brick, trivet, torch, and titanium pick
- Klyr-Fire
- Sifter, dust mask, and magazine sheet
- Dapping block and hammer
- 1.25mm hole-punching pliers
- Bentnose pliers and 2 pairs of chainnose pliers

PREPARE THE COPPER

The heart shapes average about 1 in. (2.5cm) wide, so it might be helpful to measure your wrist first to determine how many shapes you'll need to create the project. To make dapping easier, anneal all of the pieces of metal and allow them to cool. Place each piece into the dapping block, one at a time. Dome each piece **[1]**.

Punch a hole on each side of each heart shape.

When all hearts are domed, lay them out so they are in an alternating pattern of convex and concave. Clean the back of each piece and clear the hole of any Penny Brite with a small piece of wire or pick. Allow them to dry.

COUNTERENAMEL

Add a thin layer of Klyr-Fire and sift on the counterenamel. Rotate the metal to ensure even coverage. It might be challenging to get a perfect layer of enamel during the first firing, so don't worry if there are bare areas prior to firing. Carefully place the metal on the trivet and add a second layer of counterenamel, if needed. Repeat this process until the back-side of each heart is fully covered with enamel.

ENAMEL

Next, clean the front side of each heart. Coat the front side of the metal with Klyr-Fire. Once coated, use a pick to clear the holes. The pieces with the color on the convex side can be placed on the trivet and fired as usual **[2]**. However, the concave pieces need to be held over the flame

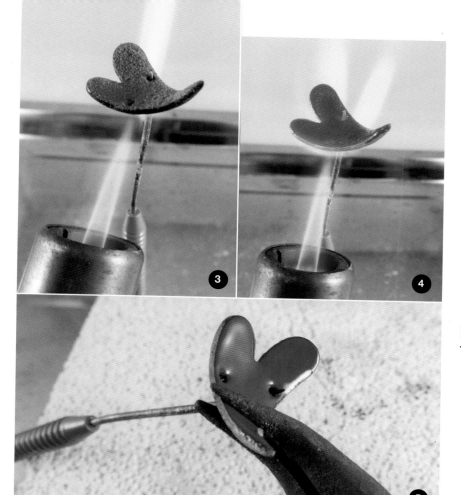

with the titanium pick. Holding the pick and metal over the kiln brick, carefully fire the heart from underneath the metal **[3, 4]**. Allow it to cool.

Once it's cool, remove the pick from the hole by slowly twisting the pick **[5]**. If the pick is covered with enamel, use a pair of bentnose pliers to crack (remove) the glass from the pick. Set the metal on the kiln brick to cool.

FINISH THE BRACELET

Using jump rings, connect the hearts together **[6]**. Add a lobster claw clasp to one end of the bracelet.

If you have trouble inserting a jump ring, you might need to use a round diamond file to make the hole opening a bit bigger: Holding the heart underwater, gently twist the file to slowly grind away any glass blocking the hole.

 TRY SOMETHING DIFFERENT

If you're not up to the challenge of creating a full-length bracelet, consider cutting a number of hearts in half and focus on a dangling pendant. It will still be just as pretty and colorful as the bracelet.

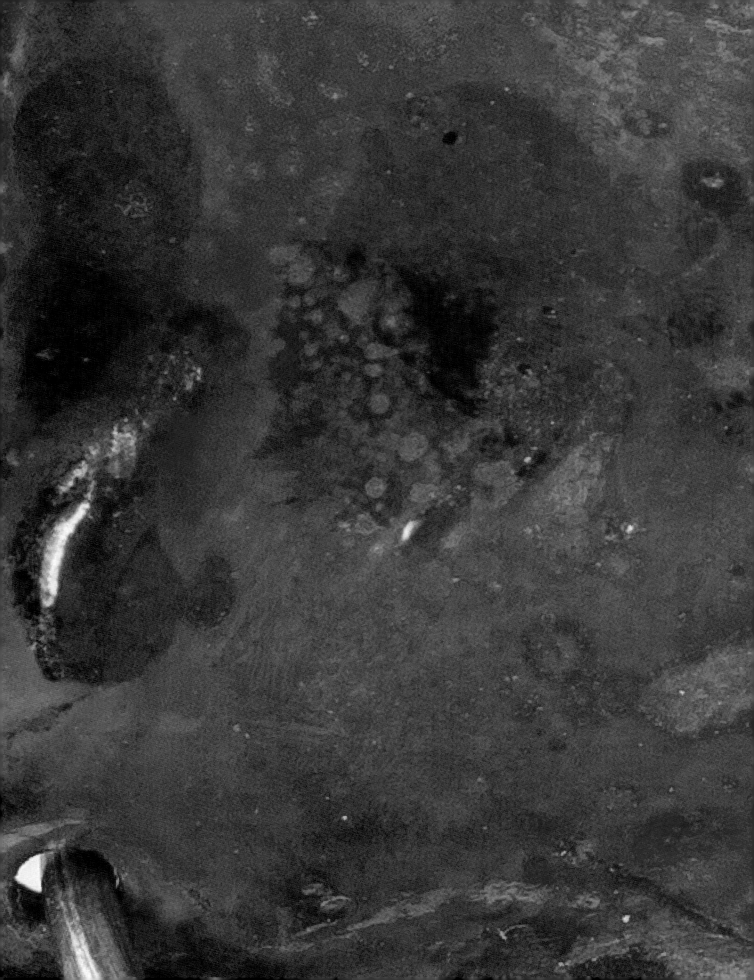

CREATING CONNECTIONS

ENAMELED YO-YO
EARRINGS

I love this project because it combines three of my favorite ways to work with enamel: formed metal, enameling paints, and riveting. There's something very therapeutic about hammering metal and it's way cheaper than therapy. I love the sgrafitto look and enamel paints offer a nice, clean appearance. As for riveting: I first learned to rivet, old-school style, using wire and a hammer. These days, new tools make riveting so much easier! Using hollow rivets allows you to create a component that, when strung correctly, can actually spin.

- 4 1-in. (2.5cm) copper disks
- 2 2mm crimps and crimp covers
- Black beading wire
- Pair of decorative earring wires
- Opaque enamels (You'll need black for counter-enamel and a color for the concave side of your design.)
- Enamel paint
- Klyr-Fire

- Penny Brite, old toothbrush, and small towel
- Kiln brick, trivet, torch, bentnose pliers, tweezers, and titanium pick
- Scalex with small paintbrush
- Sifter, dust mask, and magazine sheets
- Dapping block, bench block, and hammer
- Riveting tool with two 1⁄16-in. (2mm) rivets
- Permanent marker
- Crimping pliers

PREPARE THE METAL

To make doming easier, anneal all four copper disks. Allow them to cool, then place each piece, one at a time, into the dapping block. Dome each piece and set aside.

Next, place the pieces on a bench block and lightly tap the center of each piece to form a flattened surface. This allows the components to sit flat against each other as well as sit flat on the trivet. Once slightly flattened, find the center of each piece and mark with a permanent marker. (Use a ruler as a guide to pinpoint the center of each piece.) Place each piece into the hole-punching side of the riveting tool. Carefully screw down until a hole is punched **[1]**. Unscrew and set the dome aside. Repeat for each dome.

Clean the back (convex side) of each piece and clear the hole of any Penny Brite with a small piece of wire or the pick.

COUNTERENAMEL

Apply Scalex to the flattened area on the back of each dome **[2]**. Once dry, add a thin layer of Klyr-Fire to the back side **[3]** and sift on the counterenamel **[4]**. Try and avoid covering the flattened section. Rotate the metal while sifting to ensure even coverage. If the flattened section of the metal is covered with enamel, use a small paintbrush to remove the enamel before firing. It can be challenging to get a perfect layer of enamel while counterenameling, so don't worry if there are bare areas. Carefully place the metal on the trivet and fire **[5]**. Repeat until the backside is fully covered with counterenamel.

ENAMEL

Next, clean the inside (concave side) of each piece. Apply Klyr-Fire and sift the base color of enamel onto the inside of the dome **[6]**. There are two ways to fire the project: You can place the domed piece on an inverted steel trivet and fire until fused or use a titanium pick to clear the center hole. Remove the pick and rest the metal on the tip of the pick. Holding the pick and metal over the kiln brick, carefully fire the enamel from underneath the metal. Once fired and cool, remove the pick from the hole by slowly twisting the pick from the project. If the pick is covered with enamel, use a pair of bentnose pliers to crack (remove) the glass. Set the dome on the kiln brick to cool.

ENAMEL PAINT

Once cool, add a thin layer of enamel paint to the concave side of the metal and allow it to dry thoroughly **[7]**. Next, use the titanium pick to drag thin lines throughout the paint, removing any excess paint flakes as you work **[8]**. Once the design is complete, fire again until the paint is set **[9]**. Remove the dome from the pick and set aside. Repeat with the remaining pieces of metal.

FINISH THE EARRINGS

Lay both components back to back and insert the hollow rivet pin through the bottom. The head of the rivet pin should be on the bottom. Place the component in the riveting part of the tool and slowly twist the handle down onto the pin. Continue to twist until the pin is splayed over the center of the piece. Don't overtwist **[10, 11]**.

Cut a 6-in. (15cm) piece of beading wire and center a component. Bring both wire ends up above the component through a crimp tube. Draw one of the ends back through the crimp tube, and crimp. Trim the excess wire and cover with a crimp cover. Attach an earring wire to the loop. Repeat to make a second earring.

BULLSEYE
RING

I've always been fascinated by the simplicity of the bullseye design. This project is especially fun, because you can take what is so often a two-dimensional design and breathe a little life into by doming the individual disks that make up the piece. This particular piece also allows you to play with color. You can match the colors, keeping them within the same color family, or go for bold, contrasting colors. Whatever you decide, your finished piece will be right on target!

YOU'LL NEED

- 2 or 3 18-gauge copper disks: 1-in. (2.5mm), ¾-in. (1.9cm), and ¼-in. (6mm)
- Adjustable brass ring blank
- Riveting tool with ¹⁄₁₆-in. rivet
- Opaque enamels (Black for counterenamel and one to three colors for the concave side of your design.)

- Penny Brite, old toothbrush, and small towel
- Permanent marker and ruler
- Klyr-Fire
- Kiln brick, trivet, torch, bentnose pliers, diamond file, and titanium pick
- Sifter, dust mask, and magazine sheets
- Dapping block

PREPARE THE METAL

To make doming easier, anneal all three pieces of metal. Allow to cool, then place each piece, one at a time, into the dapping block. Dome each piece individually **[1]**.

Find the center of each piece and mark with a permanent marker. Finding the center can be challenging at first, but consider using a ruler as a guide to assist in pinpointing the middle of each piece. The riveting tool comes with two bases for hole punching, a flat base and a ring base. Replace the flat base with the ring base and then place each piece into the riveting tool. Carefully screw down until the piece is punched **[2]**. Unscrew and set the metal aside. You'll also need to punch a hole in the center of your ring blank. Repeat to punch a hole in each dome.

COUNTERENAMEL

Clean the back (convex side) of each piece and clear the hole of any Penny Brite with a small piece of wire or pick. Once dry, add counterenamel to the largest piece only. The other two pieces don't have counterenamel, because they are significantly smaller. Add a thin layer of Klyr-Fire to the back side of the largest disk **[3]** and sift on the counterenamel **[4]**. Rotate the metal to ensure even coverage. It can be challenging to get a perfect layer of enamel during the counter-enameling fire, so don't worry if there are bare areas prior to fire. Carefully place the metal upside down on the trivet and fire **[5]**. Repeat this process until the backside of the largest piece is fully covered with counterenamel.

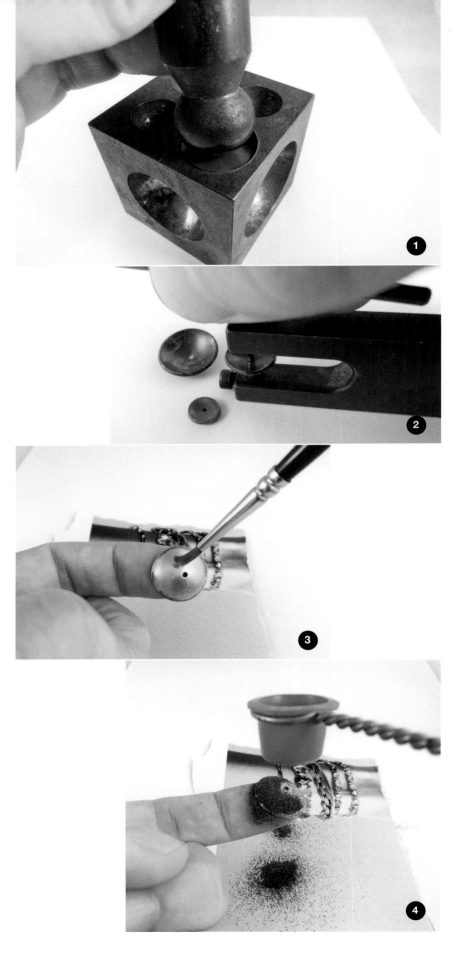

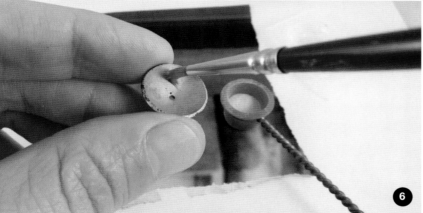

Next, clean the inside (concave side) of the each piece, beginning with the largest piece. Repeat to sift enamel onto the inside of the metal **[6]**. Once coated, use a titanium pick to clear the center hole. To avoid creating divots in the backside of your piece, fire the largest piece while it rests on the tip of the pick **[7]**. Holding the pick and metal over the kiln brick, carefully fire from underneath the metal.

Once fired, remove the pick from the hole by slowly twisting the pick from the project **[8]**. If the pick is covered with enamel, use a pair of bentnose pliers to crack (remove) the glass from the pick. Set the metal on the kiln brick to cool.

For the other two domes, simply add enamel to the concave side of the metal and set them aside to cool. Fire these two pieces, concave side up, on the stainless steel trivet. Once all pieces are fired and cool, use a small diamond file to clean the edges of the domes to remove any enamel or firescale **[9]**.

FINISH THE RING

Rinse, then dry and stack the three pieces on top of the ring blank. Insert the rivet through the assembly from the bottom of the ring blank **[10]**. The head of the rivet should be inside the ring. Place your ring into the riveting part of the tool, and slowly twist the riveting handle down onto the rivet **[11]**. Continue to twist until the rivet is flared over the center of the bullseye. Avoid over-twisting, as this can crack the glass at the center of the design. Once the rivet is set, it is ready to wear!

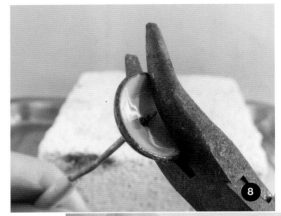

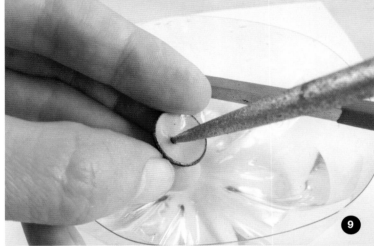

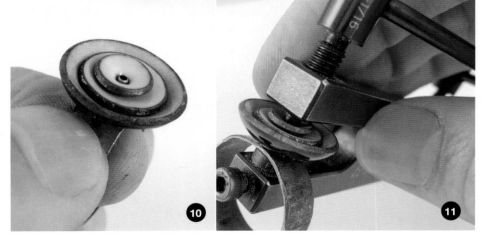

 TRY SOMETHING DIFFERENT

This is an incredibly versatile design, perfect for pendants and lightweight enough for earrings. If you want to create a different finished project instead of a ring, you'll need to punch a hole at the top of the largest copper piece. Alternatively, you can rivet your bullseye project to a leather bracelet for a bold statement.

STARBURST
CUFF

I love leather. I love riveting. So you can imagine how I feel about this riveted leather bracelet. You can rivet just about any enameled piece to a leather bracelet, but I'm particularly fond of this starburst design using the sgraffito technique. The colors and the bold contrast between painted enamels and Titanium White really help the colors come alive.

YOU'LL NEED

- 9–12 18- or 20-gauge copper disks (match diameter to width of leather bracelet)

- Adjustable pre-finished leather bracelet

- Riveting tool with one 1/16-in. (2mm) rivet for each enameled component

- Opaque enamel (I used Titanium White.)

- Counterenamel (I used Black.)

- Enamel paints in yellow, orange, red, blue, and green (or any colors you like; you can even create your own by mixing the paints.)

- Penny Brite, old toothbrush, and small towel

- Kiln brick, cross-locking tweezers, torch, diamond file, and titanium pick

- Small mesh sifter

- Permanent marker

PREPARE THE METAL

Find the center of each copper circle and mark with a permanent marker. The riveting tool comes with two bases for hole punching, a flat base (for riveting), and a punching base. Insert the metal into the punching base, and carefully screw it down until the piece is punched **[1]**. Unscrew and set the disk aside. Repeat to punch a hole in each disk. Punch corresponding holes in the leather where you would like to add the components **[2]**.

Clean the back of each disk and clear the hole of any Penny Brite with a small piece of wire or a pick.

COUNTERENAMEL

Add counterenamel to all disks. Set them on the kiln brick to cool.

ENAMEL

Add white enamel to the front of each disk. Fire and let them cool. Paint each disk with a different color of enamel paint and let dry **[3]**. Use a titanium pick to scratch a starburst design on the front **[4]** (see "Scratch Art Pendants," p. 24). Fire until the enamel is glossy **[5]**. Let it cool.

Use a small diamond file to clean the rims of the circles to remove any enamel or firescale. Rinse, then dry and prepare to rivet the leather.

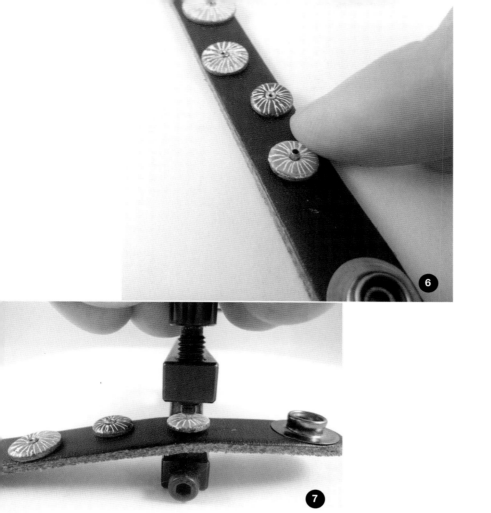

FINISH THE BRACELET

Pick a hole on the leather bracelet and then insert the rivet, bottom to top. Use a pick to open the hole in the leather if it is too tight. The head of the rivet should be on the inside of the bracelet. Place your metal component on top of the rivet **[6]** and then put the assembly into the riveting part of the tool. Slowly twist the riveting handle down onto the rivet **[7]**. Continue to twist until the rivet is splayed over the center of the metal. Avoid overtwisting, as this can crack the glass at the center of the design. Once the rivet is set, remove the bracelet and continue until all of the disks are in place **[8]**.

 TRY SOMETHING DIFFERENT

Most enameled components can be riveted to leather. You can keep it simple with a single piece (yes, the components from the "Bullseye Ring," p. 97, look amazing on leather), or you can add several pieces to a leather cuff.

RAINBOW FRINGE
BROOCH

This is a great project because it not only allows you to practice riveting skills, but you can also learn how to blend transparent enamels with opaques to create new colors. There are times when I use enameling paints if I want to make a new color such as indigo, but it is quite simple to do it with transparent colors as well!

YOU'LL NEED

- 2–3 1-in. (2.5cm) 18-gauge copper squares
- 1½x⅜-in. (3.8x1cm) 18-gauge copper rectangle
- 7 5mm jump rings
- 20mm pin back
- Opaque and transparent enamels (I used Orient Red, Pumpkin Orange, Titanium White with overcoat of Egg Yellow Transparent, Hunter Green, Cobalt Blue with overcoat of Savor Purple Transparent, and Grape Purple.)
- Counterenamel (I used Black.)

- Water bowl, Penny Brite, old toothbrush, small towel
- Black, fine-point permanent marker and tape
- Kiln brick, trivet, torch, bentnose pliers, metal file, and fine-point tweezers
- Sifter, dust mask, and magazine sheets
- Hole-punching pliers
- Riveting tool with ¹⁄₁₆-in. (2mm) rivet
- French shears
- Hammer and bench block
- 2 pairs of chainnose pliers

PREPARE THE SQUARES

Anneal all of the copper squares—this process makes them easier to cut. Place the squares on the kiln brick and bring them to a bright red glow. Allow them to cool, then use a pair of fine-point tweezers to quench them in a bowl of water. Dry the squares.

Use a fine-tip permanent marker to divide the squares into seven rectangles **[1]**. Use the shears to cut the rectangles **[2]**. They will curl as you cut them, so place them on a bench block and use a hammer and bench block to flatten them back out.

Punch a hole on one end of each rectangle, and gently file the corners to remove any sharp or rough edges.

COUNTERENAMEL THE SMALL RECTANGLES

Clean the backside of each small rectangle. Counterenamel the backside of all the rectangles with black enamel. Before firing, clean out the holes in the metal. Fire the counter-enamel and allow to cool. Remove metal from the trivet, allow the metal to cool completely, and clean the front side.

ENAMEL THE SMALL RECTANGLES

Add a different color to the front of each rectangle, repeating the same sifting process as with the counter-enamel **[3]**. In order to get the brightest yellow, first fire a base coat of Titanium White, then add a layer of Transparent Egg Yellow. Indigo also involves the use of a transparent on top of an opaque: First, fire a base coat of Cobalt Blue and then add a

NOTE

These smaller, rectangular shapes can be tricky to position on the trivet, so practice placing the unfired metal pieces on the trivet before adding enamel. If they are not placed correctly, they have a tendency to fall off during the firing process.

layer of Savor Purple. Once all of the pieces are fired, file the edges and if desired oxidize the pieces to darken the exposed edges.

Determine where the brooch component will rest on the back of the piece. First, place a piece of tape over the pin to avoid poking yourself. Draw a hole on the metal, and use the riveting tool to punch your rivet hole **[4, 5]**. Punch a matching hole in the brooch component as well **[6]**. Next, line up the fringe pieces underneath the large (unfired) copper rectangle, and draw holes on the large rectangle where they will dangle. Punch the holes.

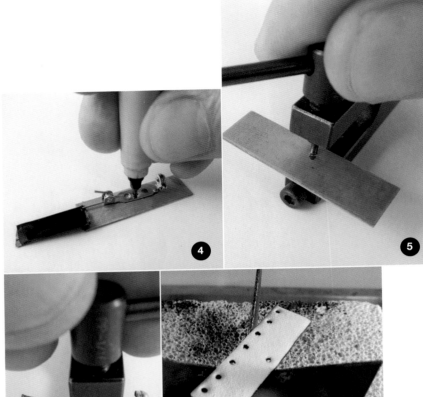

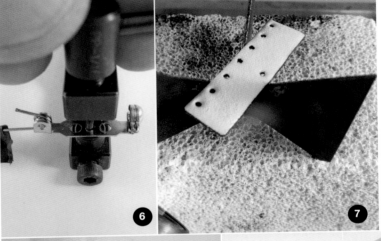

Enamel the Large Rectangle

Clean the back side of the larger rectangular piece and add the counter-enamel. Use a small titanium pick to remove enamel from the holes. Once cool, clean the front side of the piece and add your selected color. Fire **[7]** and file the edges. If desired, oxidize the piece to darken the exposed edges.

Finish the Brooch

Use the riveting tool to add the brooch component to the backside of the larger enameled rectangle **[8]**. Use jump rings to connect the small rectangles beneath the large rectangles **[9]**.

 Try Something Different

I was inspired by the colors of the rainbow, but any color combinations will work with this project. You might also consider riveting the pin back to a different shape, as well as using different shapes for the fringe.

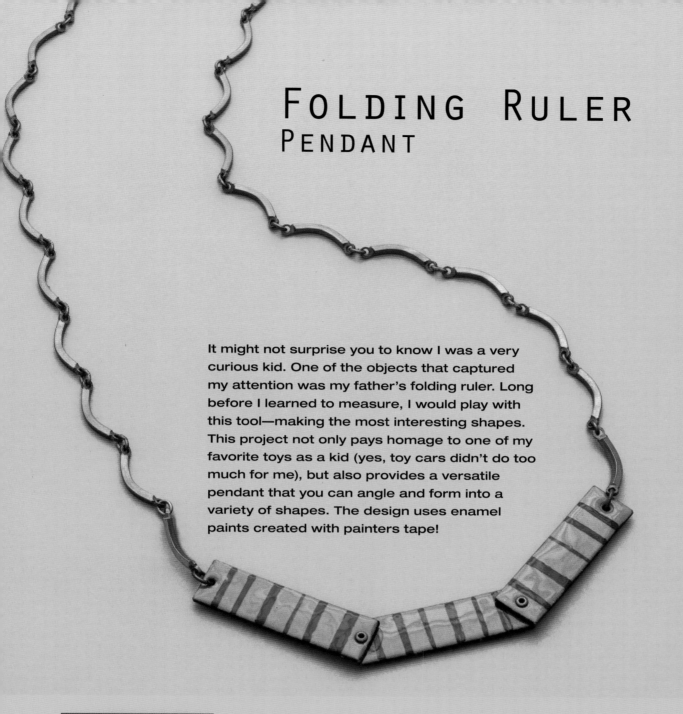

FOLDING RULER
PENDANT

It might not surprise you to know I was a very curious kid. One of the objects that captured my attention was my father's folding ruler. Long before I learned to measure, I would play with this tool—making the most interesting shapes. This project not only pays homage to one of my favorite toys as a kid (yes, toy cars didn't do too much for me), but also provides a versatile pendant that you can angle and form into a variety of shapes. The design uses enamel paints created with painters tape!

YOU'LL NEED

- 3 1⅜x¼-in. (3.5x6cm) 18-gauge copper rectangles

- 4 6-7mm jump rings

- 12mm lobster claw clasp

- 20-in. decorative chain

- Riveting tool with two ¹⁄₁₆-in. (2mm) rivets

- Counterenamel (I used Black.)

- Enamel (I used Stump Gray.)

- Enameling paint (I used Blue.)

- Small paintbrush

- Painter's tape and scissors

- Penny Brite, old toothbrush, and small towel

- Kiln brick, trivet, cross-locking tweezers, torch, diamond file, and titanium pick

- Small mesh sifter

PREPARE THE METAL

Punch a hole at the end of each rectangle. The holes should be aligned with each other, so the rectangles align when extended into a single line. The riveting tool comes with two bases for hole punching, a flat base (for riveting) and a punching base. Insert the metal into punching base and carefully screw down until the piece is punched. Unscrew and set the metal aside. Repeat for each piece.

COUNTERENAMEL

Clean the back of each piece and clear the hole of any Penny Brite with a small piece of wire or pick. Let dry. Add Black counterenamel to all pieces. Set the metal on the kiln brick to cool. Now, sift Stump Grey enamel to the front side of each piece and fire until fused.

ADD THE DESIGN

While the pieces are cooling, cut small strips of the painter's tape and set aside **[1]**. Add the painter's tape to the rectangles as shown, and press firmly **[2]**. Next, lightly brush on the Blue enameling paint, doing so in one direction for even and consistent paint coverage **[3]**. Allow the paint to completely dry before slowly peeling off the tape **[4]**. If you didn't get perfect lines, you can use a pick to remove wayward paint or simply wash off the paint and start the process over again.

Fire each piece on the trivet **[5]**. Remember, paints must go through all stages too—paint should become as glossy as the background color. Remove the rectangle from the trivet and repeat until all pieces are fired.

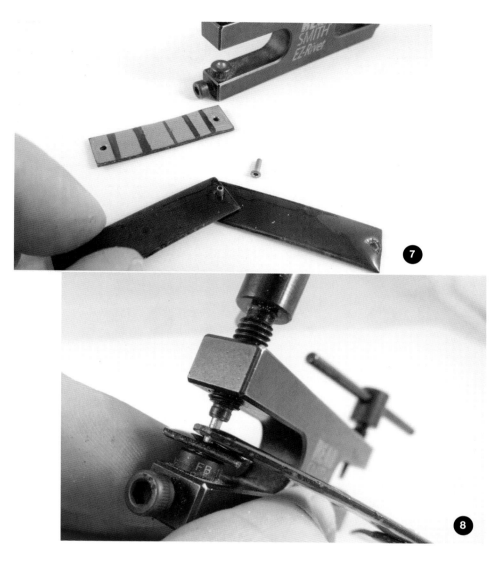

Allow them to cool, and then use a small diamond file to clean the rims to remove any enamel or firescale **[6]**. If desired, oxidize the pieces to produce a solid and blackened rim around each piece. Rinse, then dry and prepare to rivet together.

COMPLETE THE PIECE

Insert the rivet pin through the bottom of one rectangle **[7]**. The head of the rivet pin should be on the bottom. Place another rectangle on top of the pin and then into the riveting part of the tool, slowly twisting the riveting handle down onto the pin. Continue to twist until the pin is splayed over the center of the metal **[8]**. Avoid over-twisting, as this can crack the glass at the center of the design. The connection should be tight enough so you can adjust the rectangles if desired. Once the rivet is set, remove the project and rivet the other section.

Next, add the "pendant" to the center of the 20-in. (51cm) chain with two jump rings. Then attach a 12mm lobster claw clasp to one end and a 6-7mm jump ring to the other end to finish the necklace.

TRY SOMETHING DIFFERENT

When I first taught enameling, I introduced students to designs created with sifted enamel over punched paper stencils. Painter's tape can be used the same way—plus, you can get crisper details when using paint. To create a stencil with painter's tape, place it on a sturdier piece of glossy paper (I use perfume insert pages from magazines) and then punch with your decorative punch. Remove the tape and place directly onto the glass, press into place, and then gently brush on the paint. Allow to dry and peel off.

Other Techniques

To finish your jewelry, you'll need to learn a few basic jewelry-making techniques. These loops and wraps will polish off your pieces nicely for beautiful necklaces, earrings, bracelets, and brooches you'll be excited to wear!

  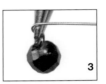

Plain loop

Trim the wire or headpin ⅜ in. (1cm) above the top bead. Make a right-angle bend close to the bead **[1]**.

Grab the wire's tip with roundnose pliers. The tip of the wire should be flush with the pliers. Roll the wire to form a half circle. Release the wire **[2]**.

Reposition the pliers in the loop and continue rolling **[3]**.

The finished loop should form a centered circle above the bead **[4]**.

Wrapped loop

Make sure you have at least 1¼ in. (3.2cm) of wire above the bead. With the tip of your chainnose pliers, grasp the wire directly above the bead. Bend the wire (above the pliers) into a right angle **[1]**.

Using roundnose pliers, position the jaws in the bend **[2]**. Bring the wire over the top jaw of the roundnose pliers **[3]**. Reposition the pliers' lower jaw snugly into the loop. Curve the wire downward around the bottom of the roundnose pliers. This is the first half of a wrapped loop **[4]**. Add chain at this point, if desired.

Position the chainnose pliers' jaws across the loop **[5]**. Wrap the wire around the wire stem, covering the stem between the loop and the top bead. Trim the excess wire and press the cut end close to the wraps with chainnose pliers **[6]**.

Opening and closing loops or jump rings

Hold the loop or jump ring with two pairs of chainnose pliers or chainnose and roundnose pliers, as shown **[1]**.

To open the loop or jump ring, bring one pair of pliers toward you and push the other pair away. String materials on the open loop or jump ring. Reverse the steps to close the open loop or jump ring **[2]**.

ACKNOWLEDGMENTS

I'd like to thank several people, but first and foremost, my parental figures (all three of them) for letting me be me!

Thank you Steve Scowden, for supporting the creative chaos—I promise to clean the garage next week. Kate Richbourg, who, as my crafting sherpa, first guided me into this jewelry-making world.

This project had a serious suppprter in Karin Von Voorhees, my first book editor at Kalmbach. She never gave up and worked with me to make this all happen. And a big shout-out to Erica Swanson, who helped make sure my personality came through the pages of this book.

Finally, if you ever been in a class with me, you know how much I thrive on the energy and enthusiasm my students give—I love being a teacher both of adults (and kids)—and it's because of my fifth-grade teacher, Marion Anderson, whose style and honesty helped make me the teacher I am today.

ABOUT THE AUTHOR

Steven James spent his childhood coloring outside the lines, peeling the wrapper off crayons, and making glue skin in the palm of his hand.

Now older, wiser, and craftier, he invites you to join in the fun. Put aside the responsibilities of your life and get back the creative connections you made as an eight-year old. A full-time elementary-school teacher, who has made appearances on the DIY and HGTV networks, Steven loves taking a break from his grade-school routine to spend a few hours with adults who will hopefully avoid picking noses, scabs, or fights and focus on getting inspired, being creative, and most importantly, having fun.

His work has appeared in magazines such as *ReadyMade* and *Bead Style,* and books from Lark and Kalmbach. He has spread his love for the handmade by developing craft ideas for TiVo, the Gap, and the San Francisco Chronicle, as well as various websites. Living by the mantra, "What are you gonna make today?" Steven hopes to spark creativity in everyone he meets, and loves teaching classes around the world.

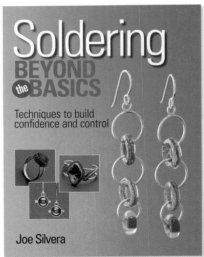